829.
3
BEO

Beowulf.

| DATE | | | |
|---|---|---|---|
| | | | |
| | | | |
| | | | |
| | | | |
| | | | |
| | | | |
| | | | |
| | | | |
| | | | |
| | | | |
| | | | |
| | | | |
| | | | |

# BEOWULF

Bloom's
## NOTES

A Contemporary
Literary Views Book

Edited and with an Introduction by
## HAROLD BLOOM

Printed and bound in the United States of America.

First Printing
1 3 5 7 9 8 6 4 2

*Cover illustration:* Art Resource

Library of Congress Cataloging-in-Publication Data

Beowulf / edited and with an introduction by Harold Bloom.
p. cm. — (Bloom's Notes)
"Books by the author of Beowulf":
Includes bibliographical references and index.
Summary: Includes information about the author of "Beowulf," thematic and structural analysis of the work, critical views, and an index of themes and ideas.
ISBN 0-7910-4053-4.
1. Beowulf. 2. Epic poetry, English (Old)—History and criticism.
[1. Beowulf. 2. English literature—History and criticism.] I. Bloom, Harold.
II. Series.
PR1585.B57 1995
829'.3—dc20
95-45110
CIP
AC

Chelsea House Publishers
1974 Sproul Road, Suite 400
P.O. Box 914
Broomall, PA 19008-0914

# Contents

# User's Guide

This volume is designed to present historical, critical, and bibliographical information on *Beowulf*. Following Harold Bloom's introduction, there appears a detailed discussion of the background of the anonymous work. Then follows a thematic and structural analysis of the work, in which significant themes, patterns, and motifs are traced. An annotated list of characters supplies brief information on the chief characters in the work.

A selection of critical extracts, derived from previously published material by leading critics, then follows. The extracts consist of early notices of the work as well as later evaluations down to the present day. The items are arranged chronologically by date of first publication. A bibliography of editions of *Beowulf* (including both the Anglo-Saxon text and English translations), a list of additional books and articles on *Beowulf*, and an index of themes and ideas conclude the volume.

---

**Harold Bloom** is Sterling Professor of the Humanities at Yale University and Henry W. and Albert A. Berg Professor of English at the New York University Graduate School. He is the author of twenty books and the editor of more than thirty anthologies of literature and literary criticism.

Professor Bloom's works include *Shelley's Mythmaking* (1959), *The Visionary Company* (1961), *Blake's Apocalypse* (1963), *Yeats* (1970), *A Map of Misreading* (1975), *Kabbalah and Criticism* (1975), and *Agon: Towards a Theory of Revisionism* (1982). *The Anxiety of Influence* (1973) sets forth Professor Bloom's provocative theory of the literary relationships between the great writers and their predecessors. His most recent books are *The American Religion* (1992) and *The Western Canon* (1994).

Professor Bloom earned his Ph.D. from Yale University in 1955 and has served on the Yale faculty since then. He is a 1985 MacArthur Foundation Award recipient and served as the Charles Eliot Norton Professor of Poetry at Harvard University in 1987–88. He is currently the editor of the Chelsea House series Major Literary Characters and Modern Critical Views, and other Chelsea House series in literary criticism.

# Introduction

HAROLD BLOOM

The Old English epic *Beowulf* may have been written during the first half of the eighth century, or it may have been composed at about the year 1000, which is the date of the manuscript. Either way, it was written in a Christian Britain, but one with many memories of the pagan past. Is *Beowulf* a Christian poem? Just barely; in any case, it has a profoundly elegiac relation to its Germanic origins. Though the nameless poet of this heroic epic must have been at least ostensibly Christian, *Beowulf* eschews any mention of Jesus Christ, and all its biblical references are to the Old Testament. The prime human virtue exalted in the poem is courage; Beowulf fights primarily for fame, for the glory of becoming the prime Germanic hero, and secondarily he battles for gain, for treasure he can give away, so as to show his largess at bestowing gifts. Grendel and his even nastier mother are descendants of Cain, but they are not described as being enemies of Christ. Even the dragon of the poem's conclusion is by no means identified with the dragon of Revelation. Perhaps aesthetic tact governs the poet of *Beowulf:* his hero's virtues have nothing to do with salvation, and everything to do with warlike courage. When Beowulf's people, at the epic's conclusion, lament the death of their lord—"They said that among the world's kings, he was the mildest and gentlest of men, most kind to his people and most eager for praise"—mildness, gentleness, and kindness are hardly Christian, since they never are exercised towards Beowulf's human enemies, and that praise for which the hero was "most eager" is purely Germanic. Since the audience of *Beowulf* was definitely Christian, what were the motives of the poet?

One valid answer may be nostalgia, most brilliantly expressed by Ian Duncan:

> As *Beowulf* progresses, the monumental records of past origins grow ambiguous and dark, from the bright mythic-heroic genealogies and creation songs of the opening, through the annals of ancient strife carved on the golden hilt from the Grendel hall, to the dragon hoard itself, a mysterious and sinister, possibly accursed relic, signifying racial extinctions. But

> Beowulf seems to recognize . . . that his affinity with the dragon has extended to a melancholy kinship. . . .

Hence the dark conclusion, where the dragon and the hero expire together. All of the poem then is a beautiful fading away of Germanic origins, presumably into the light of a Christian common day. An even subtler reading is offered by Fred C. Robinson, who sees the poem as a blend of pagan heroism and Christian regret. This double perspective does seem to be a prominent feature of *Beowulf* and reminds me of the double perspective of the *Aeneid,* a poem at once Augustan and Epicurean. But does *Beowulf* conclude with the triumph of the Christian vision? God's glory as a creator is extolled in the poem, but nowhere are we told of God's grace. Instead, there are tributes, despairing but firm, to fate, hardly a Christian power. Though the beliefs of the writer of *Beowulf* doubtless were Christian, his poetic sympathies pragmatically seem to reside in the heroic past. ❖

# The *Beowulf* Poet and Text

Scholars consider the author of *Beowulf* an immensely gifted poet, but that is all that is really known about him. His name and biographical information were not preserved, leaving the issue open to much speculation. Some critics suggest that each of the poem's three fights may have been composed by a different author and later combined by others who added the various digressive narratives, but most subscribe to the notion of a single poet.

Judging from the poem's content and style, certain elements of *Beowulf*'s composition are clear. Whether or not the poet originally produced an oral or a written composition, the work definitely follows conventions of the oral poetic tradition. While the poet obviously had knowledge of Christianity, he also draws from traditional Germanic heroic poetry passed down from minstrels. No character named Beowulf appears in any other known heroic poem, but his adventures slightly resemble those in the widely recounted "Bear's Son" tale (also called "Strong John" and "The Three Stolen Princesses"). Although the work seems most connected to Old Norse folklore, some of it is based on fact; historical records document the existence of Hygelac, king of the Geats (and Beowulf's uncle in the story), who died in 521 C.E.

The only concrete evidence of the poet's existence remains a *Beowulf* manuscript produced around 1000. Two different scribes copied the poet's work in West Saxon, an Old English literary dialect, and an early editor gave the poem its title. The only surviving copy, this manuscript was preserved in the library of Sir Robert Cotton and is currently housed in the manuscript codex Cotton Vitellius A. XV (collected with three prose stories about monsters and one poem fragment) in the British Museum. The manuscript was damaged by fire, but Icelandic scholar Grímur Thorkelin transcribed it and published an edition in 1815.

Since the early English masterpiece was published, scholars have tried to determine where and when the work could have originated. They have employed the study of archaeology, history, linguistics, and Christianity in this pursuit but still have no conclusive answers. The poetic dialect does not pinpoint a specific time or region, nor does the level of Christianity in the poem indicate a very specific period. Historical knowledge can only narrow the date of composition to anywhere between the seventh century, closer to the time the Scandinavian leaders mentioned in the story actually lived, and the ninth century, when the Danes invaded England.

Within this broad time frame, there are a few likely places where the poet could have composed his work. In identifying areas of high culture and support for the arts, scholars have named two plausible candidates: the Anglo-Saxon kingdoms of Northumbria, in northern England, and Mercia, in south-central England. Northumbria seems a possible place of origin between 673 and 735, an era known as the age of Bede, after a noted teacher and historian. The court of King Aldfrith, who reigned from 685 to 705, welcomed scholars and poets.

During the reign of King Offa II (757–796), Mercia cultivated many learned artists, making it another likely home for the *Beowulf* poet. Offa was the most powerful English king of this time, and the digression in *Beowulf* mentioning Offa, king of Angeln in the fourth century, could have been meant as a tribute to a royal patron.

Seventh-century East Anglia, with the highly developed culture of the Wuffingas dynasty (625–55), has also been judged a possibility. Archaeologists unearthed a treasure-burial at Sutton Hoo similar to the described burials of Scyld and Beowulf, and grave goods linked to royal burials in Uppsala, Sweden, have also been found that are similar to ones described in the poem. The Wuffingas dynasty and its first two kings, Wehha and Wuffa, who could have migrated from Uppsala to East Anglia, resemble the *Beowulf* names Wylfingas, Weohstan, and Wiglaf. This mystery will never be solved, but the *Beowulf* poet lives on through the undisputed greatness of his work. ❖

# Thematic and Structural Analysis

*Beowulf,* the longest Anglo-Saxon poem in existence, is a deceptively simple tale about the adventures of a sixth-century Germanic hero who fights three monsters in what is now Denmark and Sweden. Beneath this staightforward and, to a modern reader, somewhat naive plot, however, lies a highly structured work filled with historical and legendary allusions that subtly parallel, contrast with, and foreshadow the poem's action.

The poem begins with the funeral of a great king, Scyld Scefing, the legendary founder of the Danish royal dynasty (**lines 1–63**). (It will end with the funeral of another great king—Beowulf, the poem's protagonist.) According to legend, Scyld was found alone in a boat laden with treasure when he was a child. Upon his death the Danes honor him by placing his body in another treasure ship and putting the ship out to sea.

Scyld Scefing's subjects begin to call themselves the Scyldings and are well ruled by his son Beowulf (usually referred to as Beow to differentiate him from the hero of the poem). Beow, in turn is succeeded by his son Healfdene, who has four children: Heorogar, Hrothgar, Halga, and a daughter whose name has been lost but who married Onela, a Swedish (or in Anglo-Saxon terms, Scylfing) king.

Of these children, Hrothgar is especially successful in battle and becomes ruler of the Scyldings after Heorogar is killed (**lines 64–85**). Rulers at this time relied on the allegiance of warrior-retainers called thanes. Their relationship was embodied in the heroic code, which required of the thane unbounded courage in battle and absolute loyalty to the ruler. In exchange, a ruler was expected to protect and provide for his thanes (who, after all, could not support themselves if they were constantly away fighting). A ruler was supposed to share generously the wealth taken in conquest, giving lavish gifts to his thanes in reward for their services. In addition, he provided them with a mead-hall—a place to live, with food, drink, and nightly entertainment.

The elderly Hrothgar is a good ruler and builds the largest and most lavish mead-hall anyone has ever seen, calling it Heorot. Although the poet alludes to Heorot's later destruction during a war—the result of "the sharp-edged hate of [Hrothgar's] sworn son-in-law"—at this point it is a happy place where the king holds feasts and hands out treasure. *Beowulf* abounds with similar allusions to future sorrows embedded in a joyful present. These allusions, which the poet's original audience would readily recognize, serve one of the poem's primary themes: the vicissitudes of life and the impermanence of all human endeavors.

The noise and merriment of the festivities, particularly the song of a scop, or bard, praising God, proves a torment to one creature—Grendel, a powerful and evil monster who lives as an outcast on the nearby moors (**lines 86–193**). Grendel, the poem explains, is a descendant of the biblical character Cain, who killed his brother Abel and was cursed by God. All malevolent monsters are Cain's descendants; like Cain, they strive against God but ultimately in vain.

Enraged by the happy sounds coming from Heorot, Grendel waits for night to fall. Then he creeps into Heorot, seizes thirty sleeping thanes, and takes "his slaughtered feast of men to his lair." The next night, Grendel attacks again, until the frightened thanes abandon Heorot and sleep elsewhere.

For twelve years, Grendel terrorizes Heorot. Hrothgar is distraught at the deaths of his thanes, but there seems to be no appeasing the monster. Although the Scyldings use Heorot during the day, at night Grendel takes up residence in the hall. Hrothgar and his men appeal to their heathen gods—a practice that *Beowulf*'s Christian author heartily condemns as ignorance "of God . . . our protector above, / the King of Glory"—but the "night-evil" continues.

Word of Grendel eventually reaches Beowulf, a thane of the Geat king Hygelac (**lines 194–370**). (The Geats occupied what is today southern Sweden.) Strictly speaking, Grendel is no concern of the Geats. But by risking his life in a dangerous battle, Beowulf can win honor (symbolized by the gold he could expect to be given by Hrothgar) and fame—which, it was believed, was the only thing that endured beyond this ephemeral life. Beowulf resolves to destroy the monster and, gathering fourteen fellow warriors, sets off by ship for Denmark. The ship is spotted by a Scylding watchman, who hurries down to the shore to find out who the warriors are. Impressed by Beowulf's manly appearance and his explanation of why he and his men have come, the guard agrees to conduct the Geats to Heorot.

The well-armed Geats enter the mead-hall and sit down on one of the hall's many benches. They excite considerable curiosity, and Hrothgar's herald, Wulfgar, asks them who they are. Beowulf tells him and asks to speak to Hrothgar. Wulfgar, also impressed by Beowulf's appearance, encourages his king to speak to them.

Hrothgar, it turns out, knew Beowulf's father, Ecgtheow, and has heard that Beowulf has "the strength of thirty [men] / in his mighty hand-grip." He believes that God, "in the fullness of mercy," has sent Beowulf to deliver them from Grendel (**lines 371–490**). Although the author has revealed that these characters are not Christian, their religion—despite their earlier appeal to heathen gods—resembles the monotheism of the Old Testament Jews (rather than the actual religious beliefs of sixth-century Scandinavians).

Hrothgar agrees to speak with the Geats, and Beowulf introduces himself, reveals his mission, and gives an account of his previous exploits, including vanquishing a family of giants and slaughtering sea serpents. Asking Hrothgar's permission to fight Grendel, Beowulf says that, like the monster, he will forsake weapons and use only his bare hands. Expressing a decided fatalism, he declares, "Whoever death takes / will have to trust in the judgment of God." All he asks is that Hrothgar send his "war-shirt" to his king, Hygelac, should Grendel triumph. In agreeing to let Beowulf fight the monster, Hrothgar reveals that he harbored Beowulf's father after Ecgtheow had "struck up a mighty feud / . . . among the Wylfings" by killing a warrior named Heatholaf, and that Ecgtheow had sworn allegiance to him. Among Germanic warriors—as the poem's numerous accounts of blood feuds make clear—vengeance for the killing of a lord or kinsman was a moral imperative. Thus feuds begot more feuds, and a warrior without the protection of a lord was extremely vulnerable to retribution.

The Geats and Scyldings sit down to feast before night falls (**lines 491–606**). A jealous Scylding, Unferth, "who would not grant that any other man / under the heavens might ever care more / for famous deeds than he himself," tries to shame Beowulf. He asks if Beowulf is the same warrior who once lost a seven-day swimming match to a man named Breca and declares that he expects similar failure if Beowulf challenges Grendel. Beowulf reveals that he and Breca did engage in a swimming match—in full armor, no less—but he did not lose. Rather, after five days at sea, Beowulf was attacked by sea monsters. He slaughtered all nine and came to shore in Finland—quite a swim from Sweden. Beowulf then chastises Unferth, declaring, "I never have heard / such struggle, sword-terror, told about you." He goes on to recriminate Unferth—and his fellow Scylding warriors—for their lack of courage and ferocity, which has brought shame to them and made Grendel's reign of terror possible:

> "I'll tell you a truth . . . :
> never would Grendel have done so much harm,
> the awesome monster, against your own leader,
> shameful in Heorot, if heart and intention,
> your great battle-spirit, were sharp as your words.
> But he has discovered he need not dread
> too great a feud, fierce rush of swords,
> not from your people, the 'Victory-Scyldings.' "

Tonight, Beowulf declares, he will show the monster "the courage and strength / of the Geats in combat."

The Scyldings are favorably impressed by Beowulf's resolve (**lines 607–709**). Hrothgar's queen, Wealhtheow, comes forward and offers the mead cup to all the warriors, including Beowulf. Evening comes and the Scyldings retire, leaving the Geats in the hall to face Grendel. Beowulf strips himself of his armor and weapons, and his retainers go to sleep fully expecting to be killed in the night. But God, the poet asserts, has granted the Geats "comfort and help, / a weaving of war-luck."

Grendel glides into the hall, hoping to find a straggler or two (**lines 710–836**). Seeing a whole host of men, he exults in his luck, expecting to make a good meal of the lot. Beowulf is quietly watching Grendel when the monster seizes and devours a nearby Geat. Grendel then reaches for Beowulf, who grabs the monster's arm in his mighty grip. Grendel quickly realizes that he is in trouble and attempts to escape, and the two engage in a tremendous fight that, the poem asserts, would have knocked down a lesser hall.

Beowulf's men try to hack the monster with their swords, but Grendel is charmed against "all weapons of battle." Grendel cannot shake Beowulf's grasp, however, and Beowulf rips off the monster's arm at the shoulder. Mortally wounded, Grendel flees Heorot, never to return. Beowulf is left with the greater glory—and Grendel's arm, complete from the shoulder to the clawlike fingers.

Morning comes, and the Scyldings are ecstatic to find that Grendel has been vanquished (**lines 837–924**). Some Scylding warriors follow the tracks of the wounded monster, who has returned to his den under a lake in the moors. Then they ride back to Heorot, speaking of Beowulf's tremendous deed. Along the way, a scop composes a poem celebrating Beowulf's victory, thus assuring that word of the hero's deeds will survive him. The scop goes on to tell the stories of the heroic Sigemund, who slew a dragon, and the tyrannical Heremod, who killed many of his own subjects before meeting his end. The Scyldings return to Heorot as Hrothgar enters.

Upon seeing Grendel's arm, Hrothgar thanks God and promises to love Beowulf as a son (**lines 925–1062**). Beowulf recounts the events of the night before, leaving the Scyldings, especially Unferth, appropriately impressed. A tremendous feast is held, during which Hrothgar gives Beowulf and the other Geats horses, armor, and treasure, including "the largest gold collar / ever heard of on earth." That gold collar links the present with the future as the poet reveals that the Geat king Hygelac will be wearing it when he dies in battle "that time he sought trouble, stirred up a feud, / a fight with the Frisians, in his pride and daring." The grisly battlefield and the joyous celebration in the mead-hall are juxtaposed to great effect

("... warriors rifled the corpses / after the battle-harvest. Dead Geats / filled the field. Now cheers for Beowulf rose"), again emphasizing the vicissitudes of men's fortunes.

During the celebration, a scop tells the tragic tale of a war between the Danes and the Jutes (**lines 1063–1250**). This tale is especially sad because Hildeburh, the wife of the Jute king, Finn, was also the sister of the Danish king, Hnaef. (Princesses often served as "peace-weavers"—they were given in marriage to rulers of other peoples to settle conflicts.) But when war broke out between the two peoples, Hildeburh's brother and son fought on opposing sides, and both were killed. A short peace followed; then the new Danish king, Hengest, attacked the Jutes, killed Finn, and took Hildeburh back to Denmark. After the scop has finished the tragic tale of one queen, another Danish queen, Wealhtheow, speaks of the unity of her people: "Each noble here is true to the other, / every kind heart death-loyal to lord." The irony is keen, for as the poet has implied, the treachery of Wealhtheow's nephew Hrothulf will eventually tear apart her family just as Hildeburh's family was destroyed.

The ominous tone is made more explicit as the thanes settle down in Heorot for the night (**lines 1251–99**). One will be killed, the poet reports, because Grendel has a mother. As the thanes sleep, Grendel's mother comes to Heorot seeking revenge for the death of her son. Although not as strong or terrible as Grendel, she bursts into the hall and quickly kills a thane, escaping with his body—and with Grendel's arm.

Beowulf is spending the night elsewhere, but when morning comes he goes to Hrothgar's chambers and hears the bad news (**lines 1300–1382**). Hrothgar is distraught at the death of his thane, Aeschere, who was a trusted counselor. But he knows who committed the dastardly act: a female monster who had often been seen accompanying Grendel as he stalked the moors and whose lair is known to be under a lake not too distant from Heorot. Hrothgar offers Beowulf more treasure if he will go to the lake and kill the monster.

Beowulf agrees (**lines 1383–1472**). In a speech that succinctly expresses the warrior's fatalistic outlook in the pursuit of renown, Beowulf declares,

"Grieve not, wise king! Better it is
for every man to avenge his friend
than mourn overmuch. Each of us must come
to the end of his life: let him who may
win fame before death. That is the best
memorial for a man after he is gone."

Hrothgar, Beowulf, and a group of warriors set out for the lake, which is a sinister place in the middle of a foreboding landscape. When they arrive, they see signs of the previous night's carnage: The water is red with blood, and Aeschere's head is lying nearby. The lake is also seething with serpents. A Geat bowman kills one with an arrow, and the others haul it ashore with their spears; it is a gruesome, monstrous thing.

Beowulf is nonetheless undaunted and gathers his armor, including a sword, Hrunting, lent to him by a repentant Unferth (**lines 1473–1590**). *Beowulf* contains many descriptions of famed swords and their histories. In this warrior culture a well-made sword was more than a tool—it was a most prized possession, almost an object of veneration, and was passed down from generation to generation. Beowulf makes appropriate provisions for his treasure in case of his death and plunges into the water. Grendel's mother grabs him and pulls him toward her den, a cave at the bottom of the lake; although protected by his armor, he cannot draw his sword, and he is beset by serpents. However, once in the den, which is dry and free of serpents, Beowulf seizes the initiative, striking Grendel's mother with Hrunting. But the blade does not "bite through to kill"— the first time, we are told, that "a word could be said against that great treasure."

Undaunted by Hrunting's failure, Beowulf, "battle-furious," grabs Grendel's mother by the shoulder and throws her to the floor. She quickly gets up, knocks him down, and sits on him, pulling out her knife to finish him off. But her blade cannot penetrate his armor, and Beowulf regains his feet, at which point, the poet asserts, God decides the struggle in favor of good. Looking around, Beowulf spots a large ancient sword, "longer and heavier than any other man / could have carried in the play of war-strokes." He grabs this "shearer of life-threads," draws it, and strikes Grendel's mother. The sword slices through her neck, killing her. The cave is then illuminated by a light of mysterious origin, "even as from heaven comes the shining light / of God's candle." Using this light, Beowulf explores the den and finds Grendel's body, which he decapitates.

Meanwhile, the warriors standing around the lake see a tremendous amount of blood in the water and conclude that Beowulf has been killed (**lines 1591–1639**). The Scyldings return home, while the Geats maintain a mournful vigil. Beowulf, however, is experiencing even stranger happenings. The blood from the monsters begins to melt the sword "in battle-bloody icicles" until Beowulf is left with only the jeweled hilt. Taking the hilt and Grendel's head, he leaves the den, rises to the surface of the lake, and swims to shore. His men are overjoyed to see him alive, and they return to Heorot, four of them carrying Grendel's oversized head on a spear.

At Heorot, Beowulf recounts his adventure and presents Hrothgar with the sword hilt (**lines 1640–1884**). The king praises Beowulf for his valor but urges him not to become like Heremod, who began his career an illustrious warrior and ended it a parsimonious tyrant. In a sermonlike speech Hrothgar declares that a hero whom God permits to "travel far in delight"—that is, to enjoy happiness and pleasure for a long time—can easily assume that his good fortune will last forever. His "portion of arrogance / begins to increase," and, as he succumbs to the sins of pride and covetousness, "[h]is future state"—death—"is forgotten, forsworn, and so is God's favor." Hrothgar implores Beowulf to "[g]uard against that awful curse . . . and choose the better, eternal gains." For though his "fame lives now," "sickness or war . . . or sword's swing / thrown spear, or hateful old age" will one day level Beowulf, just as he, Hrothgar, has been humbled by the twelve years of suffering and sorrow Grendel brought him. After Hrothgar's speech, a feast is served, and when night falls, the guests sleep peacefully in Heorot.

The next day Beowulf returns Hrunting to Unferth with thanks and takes his leave of Hrothgar. The two swear friendship, and Hrothgar gives Beowulf many gifts. With tears running down his face, the old king clasps Beowulf's neck and kisses him, expecting "that never again would they look on each other / as in this brave meeting." The Geats return to their ship, load their treasure, and set sail.

They quickly reach their lord's lands (**lines 1885–1962**). The poem praises their hall; their king, Hygelac; and especially their young and generous queen, Hygd, who is compared favorably with Modthrytho, a fourth-century queen who in her youth had any thane who looked at her face in the daytime put to death.

Beowulf and his men sit with Hygelac in his hall, and Beowulf recounts his adventures, praising Hrothgar's hospitality (**lines 1963–2199**). Beowulf also discusses the hostilities between Hrothgar's Danes and the Heathobards, a people from southern Denmark. Hrothgar is planning to have his daughter, Freawaru, marry the Heathobard prince Ingeld, in order to ensure peace between the two peoples. But Beowulf is not convinced that their enmity can be overcome by such a marriage. (His caution, as the poem's original audience would know, is justified. In 520, Ingeld attacked and burned Heorot before being routed by the Danes.)

Beowulf then brings in the treasure he was given by Hrothgar and presents it to Hygelac. In sharing his booty with his king—as in his conduct on the battlefield and in the mead-hall—Beowulf shows himself to be a paragon of virtue, the poet maintains. He is "ever loyal" to Hygelac, his lord and kinsman, and generous toward Hygelac's queen, Hygd, giving her the gold necklace that Wealhtheow had bestowed on him. He has gained renown in battle but has "no savage mind"—he never kills "comrades in drink," reserving for its appropriate use on the battlefield "the gift / that God [has] given him, the greatest strength / that man ever had." Yet in his youth, the poet reveals, Beowulf had shown no signs of future greatness (which calls to mind the humble origins of Scyld Scefing). In fact, the Geats "all were convinced he was slow, or lazy, / a coward of a noble." As a result "he got little honor, / no gifts on the mead-bench from the lord of the [Geats]."

Now that he has proven his mettle, however, Beowulf receives ample reward from Hygelac, who gives him his father's gold-covered sword—the most prized among the

Geats—as well as land, a hall, and a throne of his own. Beowulf is now a lord.

Several years pass, and Hygelac is killed in battle (**lines 2200–2277**). His son, Heardred, is also killed, and the kingdom passes to Beowulf. Beowulf's rule is a prosperous time that lasts fifty years, until a fugitive stumbles into a vaulted barrow filled with treasure and—while its guardian, a dragon, sleeps—makes off with a precious cup.

Under the dragon's watchful eye, the hoard—the combined wealth of a people destroyed by war—had lain undisturbed for three hundred years (**lines 2278–2311**). But now, as the fugitive brings the cup back to his lord as a peace offering, the dragon awakes, sees the intruder's footprints, and, checking his treasure, realizes that he has been robbed.

Though the dragon (who is not presented as a particularly intelligent creature) has no idea what the treasure is and certainly cannot use it, the theft angers him. That night he seeks retribution, burning houses, including Beowulf's hall, the "gift-throne of the Geats" (**lines 2312–2344**). To Beowulf, this causes "great anguish, pain deep in mind"—in large part because he fears that it might be divine punishment for some sin he has committed. Though filled "with dark thoughts strange to his mind," he promptly readies himself to battle the beast. Realizing that the traditional wood shield will be of little use against the dragon's flames, he orders a special shield of iron made. This will not be enough to save him—for, as the poet reveals, Beowulf is destined "to reach the end of his seafaring days, / his life in this world, together with the serpent."

As in earlier days, when he singlehandedly fought Grendel and Grendel's mother, the old Beowulf scorns the notion of approaching his enemy "with troops, with a full army"; having "endured / much violence before, taken great risks / in the smash of battles," he does not fear the dragon.

At this point, the poem reflects upon the highlights of Beowulf's illustrious career before he became king (**lines 2345–2509**). After the battle in which Hygelac was killed (which took place in Frisia, in what is now the Netherlands),

Beowulf swam back to southern Sweden, carrying as trophies the armor of no less than thirty warriors he had slain. He so impressed Hygd that she offered him the throne over her own son, Heardred; the ever-noble Beowulf turned her down, however, and supported Heardred "among his people with friendly wisdom, / kept him in honor, until he grew older, / [and] could rule the Geats." When a usurper, Onela, seized the Scylfing throne and exiled the rightful heirs, Eanmund and Eadgils, Heardred gave them refuge, and Onela attacked his hall and killed Heardred and Eanmund in retaliation. Beowulf then became the Geat king and supported Eadgils in his successful attempt to retake the Scylfing throne.

"And so he survived," the poet says, "every encounter, every awful conflict, / heroic battles, till that one day / when he had to fight against the worm [dragon]." Having heard how the feud with the dragon began, Beowulf sets out for the dragon's lair with eleven retainers, guided reluctantly by the fugitive who had stolen the cup (**lines 2510–2601**).

When they reach the lair, Beowulf—his spirit "sad, / restless, death-ripe"—speaks to his men of events important to his life and to the history of the Geat people. Central to this speech are the concepts of vengeance and honor. Beowulf recounts the story of how Haethcyn, his uncle, accidentally killed his brother Herebeald—an act made all the more horrible because it could not be avenged, as that would involve murdering a kinsman. Brokenhearted, Hrethel—who was Haethcyn and Herebeald's father as well as the king of the Geats—died, and the Scylfings seized the opportunity to attack the Geats (which presumably will happen again after Beowulf's death). "My kinsmen and leaders avenged that well," Beowulf says, though in the battle Haethcyn, who had assumed the Geat throne, was killed. The next day "the third brother," Hygelac, "brought full vengeance / back to the slayer" when Ongentheow, the Scylfing king, was killed. Beowulf then touches on the exploits he performed in service to Hygelac, including his slaying of the champion of an enemy people, the Hugas, with his bare hands. "I wish even now," he declares, "to seek a quarrel, do a great deed."

He insists on fighting the dragon alone and commands his men to wait nearby. Although this demonstrates that Beowulf has not lost his valor or desire for renown, some commentators view it as an essentially irresponsible act, an example of the kind of pride Hrothgar had warned him against years before. For Beowulf's death, which might have been unnecessary, will bring calamity to his people.

When Beowulf heads to the entrance of the dragon's lair and lets out a shout, the dragon comes out breathing flames. Beowulf's armor protects him from the fire, but when he strikes the beast, his sword fails him and the dragon is only slightly wounded. The two rush together again, and Beowulf is hurt.

In the meantime, Beowulf's men have deserted him and run off into the woods. One, however, a young man named Wiglaf, who is a kinsman of Beowulf's, remembers the favors the king has shown them and implores his comrades to come to Beowulf's aid (**lines 2602–2705**). No one responds, so Wiglaf alone takes up his sword (an old family heirloom) in Beowulf's defense—the first time the young retainer has fought for his lord. As Wiglaf joins Beowulf, the dragon charges again and burns up the thane's wooden shield. Wiglaf takes refuge behind Beowulf's shield while Beowulf strikes the dragon with all his strength—only to have his sword shatter on the dragon's skull.

The dragon charges again, biting Beowulf with his huge teeth and burning him with his fire. But Wiglaf proves resolute, and despite the flames, he strikes the dragon. His blow lessens the dragon's fire, giving Beowulf the chance to pull out his knife and deliver the killing stroke to the dragon's belly.

The dragon is vanquished, but Beowulf has been fatally wounded, for the dragon's bite is poisonous (**lines 2706–2820**). Wiglaf washes Beowulf's wounds, and the king, recognizing that he will soon die, laments the fact that he has no son to take his place. He professes joy in his fifty-year reign, however, for during this time no foreign ruler had dared to "seek out a battle, / make any onslaught, terror, oppression, / upon Geatish men." Nor had Beowulf sought any intrigue, sworn deceitful oaths, or harmed his kin. Just as he had previously been an ideal thane, Beowulf, it seems, has been an ideal ruler.

Beowulf now directs Wiglaf to bring out some of the dragon's treasure—so that he "may more easily give up [his] life / and the dear kingdom that [he has] ruled long." Wiglaf obeys, but by the time he returns, Beowulf has lost consciousness. Wiglaf revives him with some water, and Beowulf, seeing the treasure, declares,

> "I give thanks aloud to the Lord of all,
> King of Glories, eternal Ruler,
> for the bright treasures I can see here,
> that I might have gained such gifts as these
> for the sake of my people before I died."

With his last breaths, he directs Wiglaf "to watch / the country's needs" and gives instructions for his funeral and for the creation of a large barrow on a cliff to serve as his memorial. Then he gives Wiglaf (who is the last of the Waegmundings, a family to which Beowulf also belongs) his gold necklace, helmet, rings, and mail-shirt. After observing that fate has swept away all his noble kinsmen and he must follow, Beowulf dies.

Wiglaf is saddened by his lord's death, although the poem points out that Beowulf performed an important service to his people by killing the dragon (**lines 2821–3027**). Wiglaf returns to the cowardly retainers, accusing them of being ingrates and predicting that their ignominy will haunt them for the rest of their lives. He then sends a messenger to go among the Geats and tell everyone of Beowulf's death. The messenger does so, predicting that their enemies—especially the Scylfings—will attack them now that their protector is gone and summarizing the feud between the Geats and Scylfings. The Geats gather to see Beowulf and the dragon, whose treasure is revealed to have been cursed (**lines 3028–3182**). Wiglaf leads some of the Geats into the dragon's cave, where they gather treasure to bury with Beowulf. They then push the dragon's body into the sea. Beowulf's people bury the remains from his funeral pyre, along with all the treasure, in the memorial barrow they construct. They bemoan the loss of their leader, who was "of the kings in this world, / the kindest to his men, the most courteous man, / the best to his people, and the most eager for fame." ❖

—Mary B. Sisson

(In Old English poetry, each line was divided into two halves, which were separated by a pause, or caesura. For the sake of typographical simplicity, the caesura has not been rendered here. All quotations are from Howell D. Chickering, Jr.'s 1977 translation.)

# List of Characters

*Beowulf,* the hero of the poem, is an ideal warrior. Strong, brave, and always honorable and loyal to his kinsmen, he has an illustrious career, first as a warrior, then as a lord, then as king of the Geats. Beowulf's courage and skill help him vanquish Grendel, Grendel's mother, and the dragon, but this last victory costs him his life.

*Grendel* is a monster who looks somewhat like a man but is huge and eats people. He terrorizes Heorot, Hrothgar's mead-hall in Denmark, for twelve years, killing anyone who spends the night in the hall. Grendel is charmed against weapons but meets his match in Beowulf, who dismembers him with his powerful grip.

*Grendel's mother,* a smaller version of Grendel, attacks Heorot to avenge Grendel's death. Beowulf kills her with a magical ancient sword he finds in her lair.

*Hrothgar,* the king of the Scyldings or Danes, is a wise and generous ruler but is too old to protect his people from Grendel and Grendel's mother. (When Beowulf is an old king, he will face a similar challenge.) After Beowulf defeats the two monsters, Hrothgar gives him sage advice about the vicissitudes of life and the dangers of pride.

*The dragon* is a fire-breathing, snakelike monster that ultimately kills Beowulf, although it dies in the process. Unlike Grendel and his mother, the dragon is not particularly intelligent.

*Unferth,* a thane in Hrothgar's court, challenges Beowulf's accomplishments and is soundly chastised by him. Unferth eventually accepts Beowulf's superiority as a warrior and lends him his sword.

*Wealhtheow,* Hrothgar's wife, epitomizes the ideal queen in her generosity and hospitality toward thanes and guests. The hazards of her essentially diplomatic role are repeatedly expressed in tales of queens caught between warring peoples.

*Hygelac* is Beowulf's uncle and the king of the Geats. Like Hrothgar, he rewards Beowulf appropriately for his heroic actions.

*Wiglaf* is a young and inexperienced thane who is the only retainer to stand by Beowulf during his fight with the dragon. As befits an honorable thane, Wiglaf is willing to risk his life to repay his lord, who is also a kinsman, for all the gifts he has received from him. ❖

# Critical Views

[Henry Wadsworth Longfellow (1807–1882), one of the most celebrated American poets of the nineteenth century, had a lifelong interest in medieval literature. Late in life he translated Dante's *Divine Comedy* (1867). In this extract, Longfellow comments upon the simplicity of *Beowulf* in both its narrative and its style.]

One of the oldest and most important remains of Anglo-Saxon literature is the epic poem of *Beowulf.* Its age is unknown; but it comes from a very distant and hoar antiquity; somewhere between the seventh and tenth centuries. It is like a piece of ancient armor; rusty and battered, and yet strong. From within comes a voice sepulchral, as if the ancient armor spoke, telling a simple, straight-forward narrative; with here and there the boastful speech of a rough old Dane, reminding one of those made by the heroes of Homer. The style, likewise, is simple,— perhaps one should say, austere. The bold metaphors, which characterize nearly all the Anglo-Saxon poems we have read, are for the most part wanting in this. The author seems mainly bent upon telling us, how his Sea-Goth slew the Grendel and the Fire-drake. He is too much in earnest to multiply epithets and gorgeous figures. At times he is tedious; at times obscure; and he who undertakes to read the original will find it no easy task.
—Henry Wadsworth Longfellow, *The Poets and Poetry of Europe* (Philadelphia: Carey & Hart, 1845), p. 4

Stopford A. Brooke on Burials in *Beowulf*

[Stopford A. Brooke (1832–1916) was a leading British critic. Among his many volumes are *English Literature* (1882), *Religion in Literature and Religion in Life* (1901), and *Four Victorian Poets* (1908). In this extract,

Brooke examines the burials that mark the beginning and end of *Beowulf*.]

The poem opens with an account of the forefathers of Hrothgar the Scylding, King of the Danes. He is the builder of Heorot, the hall where Beowulf contends with Grendel. Hrothgar is the second son of Healfdene, who is the son of another Beowulf than the hero of the poem; and this other Beowulf is the son of Scyld, from whom the dynasty of the Scyldings takes its name. In ancient days, so ran the legend, Scyld, when he was but a child, was drifted in an open boat to the shores of the Danes. When coming thus out of the secret of the sea the bark touched the land, the folk found the naked child lying asleep in the midst of arms and gems and golden treasure, and took him up and hailed him king. With as many treasures as he brought, with so many they sent him away when he died.

As he came alone and mysteriously out of the sea, so he passes away alone and mysteriously into the sea, and the introduction to the poem describes his burial. It is the burial of a hero who had passed into a divine being, but it is also the burial of a great sea-king, the earliest record by some hundred years—for the introduction is probably from an ancient song about Scyld—of many burials of the same kind among the Northern lords; but touched with so poetic a hand that it is first of all accounts in art as it is first in time. ⟨. . .⟩

As the poem begins with this burial, so it ends with the burial of Beowulf. His burial has nothing mythic, nothing mystic surrounding it. It might be that of an historical personage; and the contrast between the shore-burial and the sea-burial is worth making immediately. Beowulf, dead after his fight with the dragon, and his gray hair lying round his head, is borne to the top of the great cliff that overlooks the sea, to the very edge, where the wanderers on the sea may hereafter mark his lofty barrow. The cliff has its own name. Men saw from its height the whales tumbling in the waves, and called it Whale's Ness (Hrones-naes). There then the folk of the Geats made ready a funeral pyre, firm-fixed on the earth, and they hung it with helms and with shields of the war-host, with shining shirts of battle, as the hero had asked of them. ⟨. . .⟩

This was the burning; after the burning the barrow is raised; and it shall be told at the end how the people of the Weders built up on the point of the Ness a mound, high and broad, to be seen from far by the sailors whom Beowulf loved. There is yet another burial told of in the poem. The bard at Hrothgar's table sings of the death of Hnaef, kinsman of Hildeburh (perhaps her brother), and of the burning of Hildeburh's son on the same pyre as Hnaef. "The bloodstained battle-sark, the golden helm, the boar crest, iron-hard, were piled on the wood; and, with the two chieftains, many another Ætheling who had fallen, writhing on the field of slaughter." ⟨. . .⟩

This is an inland burial, but the other two are by the sea; and the sea-note struck thus at the beginning and close of the poem is heard constantly sounding through its verse. The men are sea-folk. Beowulf in his youth is a sea-rover, a fighter with sea-monsters, a mighty swimmer of the sea. All the action is laid on the sea-coast. The inland country, not the sea, is the unknown, the terrible. Grendel and his dam are more sea-demons than demons of the moor. Their cave is underneath the sea. Nor in the last part of the poem are we without the all-prevailing presence of the ocean. The dragon lives in a cavern on the edge of the sea. The king and the dragon fight in the hearing of the waves. Beowulf's barrow, heaped high on the edge of the sea-ness, is a beacon for "those who sail through the mists of the sea." The background of all the action is the great deep—the chorus, as it were, of this story of the fates of men. Thus the ocean life, the ocean mystery, the battle with the ocean and on the ocean begin the English poetry, and they are as vivid in it now as they were in the youth of our people. The *Battle of the Baltic,* the *Fight of the Revenge,* the *Sailor Boy, Hervè Riel,* Swinburne's sea-songs, a hundred ballads, taste of the same brine and foam which the winds drove in the faces of the men who wrote *Beowulf,* the *Seafarer,* and the *Riddles* which concern the sea. Nay, more, the very temper of mind which pervades modern poetry of the sea—a mingling of melancholy and exaltation—is to be found in English poetry before the Conquest, and strange to say it is not found again, except in scattered ballads, till we reach our own century.

—Stopford A. Brooke, *The History of Early English Literature* (New York: Macmillan, 1892), pp. 26–29

♣

# W. P. Ker on the Mediocrity of *Beowulf*

[W. P. Ker (1855–1923) was a distinguished British critic and fellow of All Souls College, Oxford. He wrote *The Eighteenth Century* (1916) and edited *The Essays of John Dryden* (1900). In this extract, Ker asserts that *Beowulf* is not worthy of the praise it has received, being merely a poem about the slaying of a monster.]

A reasonable view of the merit of *Beowulf* is not impossible, though rash enthusiasm may have made too much of it, while a correct and sober taste may have too contemptuously refused to attend to Grendel or the Firedrake. The fault of *Beowulf* is that there is nothing much in the story. The hero is occupied in killing monsters, like Hercules or Theseus. But there are other things in the lives of Hercules and Theseus besides the killing of the Hydra or of Procrustes. Beowulf has nothing else to do, when he has killed Grendel and Grendel's mother in Denmark: he goes home to his own Gautland, until at last the rolling years bring the Firedrake and his last adventure. It is too simple. Yet the three chief episodes are well wrought and well diversified; they are not repetitions, exactly; there is a change of temper between the wrestling with Grendel in the night at Heorot and the descent under water to encounter Grendel's mother; while the sentiment of the Dragon is different again. But the great beauty, the real value, of *Beowulf* is in its dignity of style. In construction it is curiously weak, in a sense preposterous; for while the main story is simplicity itself, the merest commonplace of heroic legend, all about it, in the historic allusions, there are revelations of a whole world of tragedy, plots different in import from that of *Beowulf,* more like the tragic themes of Iceland. Yet with this radical defect, a disproportion that puts the irrelevances in the centre and the serious things on the outer edges, the poem of *Beowulf* is unmistakably heroic and weighty. The thing itself is cheap; the moral and the spirit of it can only be matched among the noblest authors.

—W. P. Ker, *The Dark Ages* (New York: Scribner's, 1911), pp. 252–53

# R. W. CHAMBERS ON FOLKLORE AND *BEOWULF*

[R. W. Chambers (1874–1942), a notable British critic and editor, is the author of *England Before the Norman Conquest* (1926), *Thomas More* (1935), and other volumes. In the following extract from his study of *Beowulf*, Chambers explores the relationship between *Beowulf* and folklore, in particular the popular tale of the Bear's Son.]

One particular tale, that of the Bear's Son (extant in many forms), has been instanced as showing a resemblance to the *Beowulf*-story. In this tale the hero, a young man of extraordinary strength, (1) sets out on his adventures, associating with himself various companions; (2) makes resistance in a house against a supernatural being, which his fellows have in vain striven to withstand, and succeeds in mishandling or mutilating him. (3) By the blood-stained track of this creature, or guided by him in some other manner, the hero finds his way to a spring, or hole in the earth, (4) is lowered down by a cord and (5) overcomes in the underworld different supernatural foes, amongst whom is often included his former foe, or very rarely the mother of that foe: victory can often only be gained by the use of a magic sword which the hero finds below. (6) The hero is left treacherously in the lurch by his companions, whose duty it was to have drawn him up . . .

Now it may be objected, with truth, that this is not like the *Beowulf*-story, or even particularly like the *Grettir*-story. But the question is not merely whether it resembles these stories as we possess them, but whether it resembles the story which must have been the common origin of both. And we have only to try to reconstruct from *Beowulf* and from the *Grettis saga* a tale which can have been the common original of both, to see that it must be something extraordinarily like the folk-tale outlined above.

For example, it is true that the departure of the Danes homeward because they believe that Beowulf has met his death in the water below, bears only the remotest resemblance to the deliberate treachery which the companions in the folk-tale mete out to the hero. But when we compare the *Grettir*-story, we see there that a real breach of trust is involved, for there the priest Stein leaves the hero in the lurch, and abandons the rope by which he should have drawn Grettir up. This can hardly be an innovation on the part of the composer of the *Grettis saga,* for he is quite well disposed towards Stein, and has no motive for wantonly attributing treachery to him. The innovation presumably lies in the *Beowulf*-story, where Hrothgar and his court are depicted in such a friendly spirit that no disreputable act can be attributed to them, and consequently Hrothgar's departure home must not be allowed in any way to imperil or inconvenience the hero. A comparison of the *Beowulf*-story with the *Grettir*-story leads then to the conclusion that in the oldest version those who remained above when the hero plunged below *were* guilty of some measure of disloyalty in ceasing to watch for him. In other words we see that the further we track the *Beowulf*-story back, the more it comes to resemble the folk-tale.

And our belief that there is some connection between the folk-tale and the original of *Beowulf* must be strengthened when we find that, by a comparison of the folk-tale, we are able to explain features in *Beowulf* which strike us as difficult and even absurd: precisely as when we turn to a study of Shakespeare's sources we often find the explanation of things that puzzle us: we see that the poet is dealing with an unmanageable source, which he cannot make quite plausible. For instance: when Grendel enters Heorot he kills and eats the first of Beowulf's retinue whom he finds: no one tries to prevent him. The only explanation which the poet has to offer is that the retinue are all asleep—strange somnolence on the part of men who are awaiting a hostile attack, which they expect will be fatal to them all.

—R. W. Chambers, *Beowulf* (Cambridge: Cambridge University Press, 1921), pp. 62–63

WILLIAM WITHERLE LAWRENCE ON THE USES OF HISTORY
IN *BEOWULF*

[William Witherle Lawrence (1876–1958) is the author
of *Medieval Story and the Beginnings of the Social
Ideals of English-Speaking People* (1911),
*Shakespeare's Problem Comedies* (1931), and *Beowulf
and Epic Tradition* (1928), from which the following
extract is taken. Here, Lawrence explores the historical
roots of *Beowulf.*]

The historical portion of *Beowulf* is remarkable for its fidelity to
fact. With all its elaborations, it preserves a certain restraint.
This is particularly striking when it is compared with later versions of the same material. Contrast, for example, its account of
the feuds of Danes and Heathobards with the same events in
the pages of Saxo Grammaticus, five centuries later. Although
*Beowulf* stresses the personal elements,—the ill-starred love of
the Danish princess and the Heathobard prince, the vengeance
slumbering in the heart of a Heathobard warrior for a sire once
killed by the Danes,—it obviously presents with some clear-
ness the earlier outlines of the tale. The long speech of the old
fighter who kindles the feud anew (2047–2056) is of course
pure fiction, but it enriches the tragedy, it does not disturb it.
How different is the situation in the pages of the Danish monk!
The very foundations of the story are shattered—the
Heathobards, traditional enemies of the Danes, have themselves become Danish. So in Icelandic, although the story
develops along other lines. The further events recede into the
past, of course, the greater the departure from fact. But this is
not all; there is in *Beowulf* a sobriety of temper in dealing with
history which is quite its own. The point of view of the poet is,
in general, as impartial as that of a modern historian. He has a
hero, and his work involves glorification of that hero and the
hero's people, but he gives due tribute to the greatness of
other folk. This was the usual procedure of a minstrel of the
Heroic Age, who knew of all notable men about the circle of
the seas. Since the first two adventures lie at the court of the
Danes, it is natural that their greatness and their traditions
should occupy the earlier portion of the poem. The episodes
deal chiefly with them; the longest digression, the tale of

Finnsburg, is a story of Danish heroism. But as soon as the second adventure is over, and Beowulf and his men sail back to their native land, the Danes are quite forgotten, and the new setting brings up the richest reminiscences of the Geatas and the Swedes. Meanwhile, throughout the entire epic, the poet has not forgotten other great heroes and peoples than those with whom he is directly concerned; they might be the subjects for more long tales for winter evenings, did time but serve.

Folk-tale and history are so closely interwoven, however, that we must be constantly on the alert for distortion of fact. And *Beowulf* is, after all, a story, in which the imaginative effect is of supreme importance. Fortunately, a certain amount of documentary evidence is available by which the veracity of the poem may be tested, and it is frequently possible, where this evidence does not exist, to make fairly safe guesses as to what is elaboration of actual occurrences, and what is invention pure and simple. Thus the death of Hygelac, the sovereign of Beowulf, at the hands of the Franks and their allies, is confirmed by Frankish historians, and the accession of Hygelac's son, Heardred, has antecedent probability in its favor. But the connection of Beowulf with the noble house of the Wægmundingas and his activity as king of the Geatas is probably wholly fictitious, not merely because of his folk-tale origin, but also because of the lack of events which the poet can remember, too few for the long reign of so illustrious a king. A stout fighter would surely not have played a passive rôle in the long contests with the Swedes, the hereditary foes of his people. In dealing with the realistic background, then, it is frequently wisest to take refuge in the phrase "historical or legendary." Early poetry was not concerned to separate fact from fiction. Complete accuracy of historical detail would not increase the realism or the charm of the picture of early Germanic life in *Beowulf.* The story-teller betters things for the business of poetry, and his canvas is veracious in a different way,—in its fidelity to the spirit of the age, and to manners and customs, forms of government and conceptions of duty, as they actually existed.

—William Witherle Lawrence, *Beowulf and Epic Tradition* (Cambridge, MA: Harvard University Press, 1928), pp. 23–26

## J. R. R. TOLKIEN ON HARMONY OF LANGUAGE AND STRUCTURE IN *BEOWULF*

[J. R. R. Tolkien (1892–1973) was a distinguished scholar of Anglo-Saxon literature and Merton Professor of English Language and Literature at Oxford University. His celebrated trilogy of fantasy novels, *The Lord of the Rings* (1954–55), draws heavily upon his scholarly work. In this extract from a landmark essay on *Beowulf,* Tolkien comments on the harmony of language and structure in *Beowulf.*]

In any case we must not view this poem as in intention an exciting narrative or a romantic tale. The very nature of Old English metre is often misjudged. In it there is no single rhythmic pattern progressing from the beginning of a line to the end, and repeated with variation in other lines. The lines do not go according to a tune. They are founded on a balance; an opposition between two halves of roughly equivalent phonetic weight, and significant content, which are more often rhythmically contrasted than similar. They are more like masonry than music. In this fundamental fact of poetic expression I think there is a parallel to the total structure of *Beowulf. Beowulf* is indeed the most successful Old English poem because in it the elements, language, metre, theme, structure, are all most nearly in harmony. Judgement of the verse has often gone astray through listening for an accentual rhythm and pattern: and it seems to halt and stumble. Judgement of the theme goes astray through considering it as the narrative handling of a plot: and it seems to halt and stumble. Language and verse, of course, differ from stone or wood or paint, and can be only heard or read in a time-sequence; so that in any poem that deals at all with characters and events some narrative element must be present. We have none the less in *Beowulf* a method and structure that within the limits of the verse-kind approaches rather to sculpture or painting. It is a composition not a tune.

This is clear in the second half. In the struggle with Grendel one can as a reader dismiss the certainty of literary experience that the hero will not in fact perish, and allow oneself to share the hopes and fears of the Geats upon the shore. In the second part the author has no desire whatever that the issue should remain open, even according to literary convention. There is no need to hasten like the messenger, who rode to bear the lamentable news to the waiting people (2892ff.). They may have hoped, but we are not supposed to. By now we are supposed to have grasped the plan. Disaster is foreboded. Defeat is the theme. Triumph over the foes of man's precarious fortress is over, and we approach slowly and reluctantly the inevitable victory of death.

'In structure', it was said of *Beowulf*, 'it is curiously weak, in a sense preposterous,' though great merits of detail were allowed. In structure actually it is curiously strong, in a sense inevitable, though there are defeats of detail. The general design of the poet is not only defensible, it is, I think, admirable. There may have previously existed stirring verse dealing in straightforward manner and even in natural sequence with the Beowulf's deeds, or with the fall of Hygelac; or again with the fluctuations of the feud between the houses of Hrethel the Geat and Ongentheow the Swede; or with the tragedy of the Heathobards, and the treason that destroyed the Scylding dynasty. Indeed this must be admitted to be practically certain: it was the existence of such connected legends—connected in the mind, not necessarily dealt with in chronicle fashion or in long semi-historical poems—that permitted the peculiar use of them in *Beowulf*. This poem cannot be criticized or comprehended, if its original audience is imagined in like case to ourselves, possessing only *Beowulf* in splendid isolation. For *Beowulf* was not designed to tell the tale of Hygelac's fall, or for that matter to give the whole biography of Beowulf, still less to write the history of the Geatish kingdom and its downfall. But it used knowledge of these things for its own purpose—to give that sense of perspective, of antiquity with a greater and yet darker antiquity behind. These things are mainly on the outer edges or in the background because they belong there, if they are to function in this way. But in the centre we have an heroic figure of enlarged proportions.

—J. R. R. Tolkien, "*Beowulf*: The Monsters and the Critics,"
*Proceedings of the British Academy* 22 (1936): 273–75

[Charles W. Kennedy (1882–1969) is author of *Old English Elegies* (1936) and *Early English Christian Poetry* (1952). He also translated *The Caedmon Poems* (1916) into English prose. In this extract, Kennedy investigates the connection between *Beowulf* and old Scandinavian folktales.]

The supernatural forms of Grendel and Grendel's dam are obviously derivative from folk-tale, though the *Beowulf* poet in an early passage has blurred this lineage by tracing their descent from the monstrous offspring of Cain. Grendel is unusual among folk-tale monsters in bearing a name, and the name itself furnishes a hint of his primitive derivation. The word Grendel, as Lawrence points out, can be associated with the Old English *grund,* i.e. ground, bottom, or watery depths, and it is significant that it is in just such depths that we find the lurking-place of Grendel and his mother. English place-names preserve records of localities known as *grendles mere* (the grendel's pool), *grindles bec* (the grendel's brook), and *gryndeles sylle* (the grendel's swamp). In these place-names the word *grendel* seems to be used as a generic term for a 'grendel,' or water-monster, and it is probable that the water-demons of the *Beowulf* have original derivation from the waterfall trolls of Scandinavian myth.

More directly, however, the male and female monsters of our poem, and the narrative of Beowulf's victories over them, are traceable to well-defined and recurring patterns in a familiar type of European folk-tale. Frederick Panzer in 1910 published the results of a careful study of over 200 folk-tales which have elements of resemblance to the Grendel story. These tales with all their variations of outline have enough in common, in structure and detail, to indicate general conformance to a recurring type which has come to be known as the tale of 'The Bear's Son.' The name is suggested by the bear-like attributes of the hero, who in some versions of the tale is actually the son, or the fosterling, of a bear. Vestigial traces of this element are to be noted in the *Beowulf* in the superhuman strength of the hero, and the bear-like wrestling of his fight with Grendel and later with Dæghrefn, the slayer of Hygelac.

From the varying versions of the tale of 'The Bear's Son,' something like a central frame, or outline, can be reconstructed. An aged king builds a hall or house which is nightly haunted by a demon. The elder sons of the king are unable to overcome the invader, but the youngest son, formerly held in little esteem, wrestles with the monster and wounds him. The flight of the demon is marked by a trail of blood. An episode follows in which the hero fights in an underground lair of monsters often against a male and a female. His victory over them, sometimes by use of a magic sword, frees captive maidens who return to the upper world. But the hero is abandoned by faithless companions, and must without aid contrive means of escape from the monster's home. The tale often ends with the punishment of the traitors, and the marriage of the hero with one of the rescued maidens.

Similarities in this outline to the Grendel episodes of the *Beowulf* are, of course, general rather than precise. But it seems clear that Panzer is correct in claiming that a relationship exists, and that the *Beowulf* narrative in this respect had its earliest origin in the crude substance of folk-tale. The details of similarity suggest themselves at once: the building of the hall, the nightly invasion of the monster, the fact that the hero was little esteemed in youth, the nature of the fight and the monster's wound, the trail of blood, the female monster, the fight in the cave under water, the magic sword, the desertion of the hero by comrades.

Even more specific resemblance, however, exists between the *Beowulf* and certain Scandinavian sagas. The Icelandic saga of Grettir the Strong, dating from the end of the thirteenth century, has elements which resemble the *Beowulf* material and, in the account of the fight under water, throw a revealing light on uncertainties of description in the *Beowulf* account. It is not probable that the Sandhills episode in the *Grettissaga* was based upon the *Beowulf,* but rather that both stories are independently developed from more primitive Scandinavian origins.

—Charles W. Kennedy, *The Earliest English Poetry* (New York: Oxford University Press, 1943), pp. 69–71

[Kemp Malone (1889–1971) wrote *Studies in Heroic Legend and in Current Speech* (1959) and *The Literary History of* Hamlet (1964). In this extract, Malone argues that *Beowulf* is essentially a Christian poem but that it also draws upon pagan literary tradition.]

The monkish author, devout Christian though he is, finds much to admire in the pagan cultural tradition which, as an Englishman, he inherited from ancient Germania. It is his purpose to glorify this heroic heritage, this spiritual heirloom, this precious birthright of his nation. He accomplishes his purpose by laying stress upon those things in Germanic tradition which agree with Christianity or at any rate do not clash seriously with the Christian faith. In particular, his hero in all he says and does shows himself high-minded, gentle, and virtuous, a man dedicated to the heroic life, and the poet presents this life in terms of service: Beowulf serves his lord, his people, and all mankind, and in so doing he does not shrink from hardship, danger, and death itself. In many passages the poet's own Christianity comes to the surface; most notably, perhaps, in the so-called sermon of the aged King Hrothgar, who out of the fulness of his wisdom warns the youthful hero against the sin of pride. But even here the king's words, though obviously based on Christian teaching, are not put in specifically Christian terms, and most of the time the author keeps his Christianity below the surface. Nor does he falsify Germanic paganism by leaving out those features of it inconsistent with the Christian faith. Thus he puts in the mouth of Beowulf himself the following piece of pagan wisdom:

> it is better for every man
> to avenge his friend than to mourn much.       [1384b–1385]

The poet's picture of the Germanic past is idealized but not distorted. The devil-worship of the Danes (as the medieval Christians conceived it to be) is mentioned with perfect frankness in a famous passage (lines 175ff.). Anachronisms are fewer and less serious than one would expect in a poem of the eighth century. Indeed, perhaps the most remarkable though not the most important feature of the poem is the relative high standard of historical accuracy which it maintains. The author was clearly a man learned in the traditional lore of his people, and concerned to tell the truth as he saw it.

We have seen that the earliest Christian poets of England, whether they composed in Latin or in English, took over the poetical manner traditional for the language of composition (and pagan in origin) but supplied their own matter: namely, Christian story or Christian teaching. For the matter handed down in the old pagan poetry they had no use; indeed, they objected strongly to what the old poets had to say, much though they admired and imitated their way of saying it. For illustration, I shall have to limit myself to two utterances of Alcuin, an Englishman of the eighth century best known for the help he gave Charlemagne in the so-called Carolingian revival of learning. In one of his poems, Alcuin compares the Song of Songs most favorably with the poetry of Vergil, saying,

> I urge you, young man, to learn these canticles by heart. They are better by far than the songs of the mendacious Vergil. They sing to you the precepts of life eternal; he in his wickedness will fill your ears with worthless lies. [*Carm.* 78, 5]

Alcuin condemns with equal severity the stock of traditional story drawn upon by the English scops of his day. In a letter of his he has this to say about one of these stories:

> What has Ingeld to do with Christ? Narrow is the room, and it cannot hold both. The heavenly king will have nothing to do with so-called kings, heathen and damned, because that king reigns in heaven, world without end, but the heathen one, damned, laments in hell.

This attitude toward pagan literature prevailed, on the whole, down to the rise of humanism in fourteenth-century Italy. The humanists, however, found admirable in, say, Cicero, not only his artistic skill as a writer of Latin prose, but also his philosophy of life. This widening of interest served to accentuate, in the humanists, that reverence for classical antiquity so characteristic of the Middle Ages in general. The new movement brought the cult of classicism to the verge of idolatry, and

humanistic thinking may be looked upon as the last and most
extreme phase of medieval chronological primitivism.

—Kemp Malone, *"Beowulf," English Studies* 29, No. 6
(December 1948): 162–64

## PETER F. FISHER ON CATACLYSMIC UPHEAVALS

[Peter F. Fisher, formerly a lecturer at the Royal Military
College of Canada, is the author of *The Valley of Vision:
Blake as Prophet and Revolutionary* (1961). In this
extract, Fisher maintains that *Beowulf* contains the
same cataclysmic upheavals that are found in both the
Bible and the sagas of Scandinavia.]

In the Christian tradition and in that of the Northern sagas, the
world is represented as suffering two cataclysmic upheavals—
one by water and one by fire. With the former is associated
purgation and renewal, with the latter, death and transfigura-
tion. Beowulf is, therefore, rescued from the power of the flood
in the second battle, and the imagery suitably suggests the
Biblical Deluge. The subsequent passages describing the home-
coming and the struggles connected with political and dynastic
ambitions are a prelude to the last battle. While looking forward to the fulfillment of Beowulf's prophecy regarding the
engagement of Freawaru and Ingeld and the ensuing wars, the
reader finally discovers that he is looking backward at the illustrious career of Beowulf after a reign of fifty years. This atmo-
sphere of reminiscence is interwoven with the narrative of the
depredations of the Dragon. The sudden change is striking.

> Then straightway the terror was made known to Beowulf that in
> truth his own abode, the best of buildings, the throne of the
> Geats, was melting in the surges of flame. (2324–27)

The immediate suddenness of the catastrophe overwhelms
Beowulf, for the destruction of his throne is the destruction of

the natural field of the hero's experience, and it foreshadows with dramatic irony the end of his earthly career. The pattern of his *dōm* passes before him, and he prepares to engage in his last battle.

This last battle with the fiery antagonist is in the form of an apocalypse which reveals the theme of judgment as the ordained conclusion to that of redemption. In the first encounter, the companions in the festive hall of Heorot arouse the Satanic invader by their feasting and by singing the song of Creation. Like Satan in Milton's *Paradise Lost,* Grendel journeys from his hell-world in the subterranean cave through the chaotic waters of the mere to the human world, and his journey is a vision of the incursion of the evil will into the cosmos, placed in the Christian tradition prior to the fall of Adam. This theme is specifically developed in the next episode, in which Beowulf enters the troubled waters of the mere and is seized by Grendel's dam and dragged down into the cave. From this state he is redeemed when defeat seems inevitable, and returns to enter into the joy of his lord. His redemption is followed in due time by the acquisition of kingship and finally by the apocalyptic battle with the dragon.

> And the great dragon was cast out, that old serpent, called the Devil and Satan, which deceiveth the whole world: he was cast out into the earth, and his angels were cast out with him. (Revelation xii.9)

Either in terms of the Norse myth or the Christian tradition, this is the consummation of a catastrophic vision of judgment. The tragic hero loses himself and is represented as a failure through his self-will, pride, and presumption. But although there are the overtones of sorrow, even the death of this epic hero is a triumph in the midst of apparent catastrophe.

At the close of the epic, the twelve sons of the chieftains ride about the burial mound of Beowulf to lament the king and exalt his heroic life. Their tribute recalls the beginning of the epic and its theme, and the work is thus effectively completed. It must be borne in mind that the structure of the narrative was known to the audience. This accounts for the fact that the outcome of the three mythical battles is stated, in each instance, before the actual struggle is well under way. Suspense was not felt to be important; it was the meaning of the heroic adventure which counted, and it is in the meaning, with its wealth of suggestive imagery, that the unity of the *Beowulf* is to be found. The pattern which this imagery produces is not without coherence, and it is not difficult to see the outline of an heroic achievement expressed in a way which reflects the impact of Christian ideals upon the world of the Northern saga. As in the *Iliad*, it is the story of Beowulf and the figure of Beowulf which focus the bard's complete vision of life. The hero becomes the universal type of humanity and of the life of humanity in all its greatness, in its wonder and sorrow. Achilles is described as the man of swiftest doom (ὠκυμορώτατος); for if man himself is of swift doom, the hero is the intensification of the life of the race (*Iliad* I.505). Although the story of Beowulf does not emphasize the brevity of human existence, it does emphatically concentrate on the mortal fate which conflicts with the glory of heroic achievement and yet is the basis of redemption. Beowulf is never wholly free from despair but he triumphs over it, and in this triumph the author successfully completes his theme of judgment after recounting the trials of his hero.

—Peter F. Fisher, "The Trials of the Epic Hero in *Beowulf*," *PMLA* 73, No. 3 (June 1958): 182–83

## ARTHUR GILCHRIST BRODEUR ON STRUCTURE AND ACTION IN *BEOWULF*

[Arthur Gilchrist Brodeur is the author of *The Climax of the Finn Episode* (1943) and *The Riddle of the Runes* (1977). In this extract from his book on *Beowulf*, Brodeur relates J. R. R. Tolkien's theory of the two-part structure of *Beowulf* to the action of the poem.]

Tolkien's symbolical interpretation ⟨. . .⟩—lately challenged by T. M. Gang and ably defended by Adrien Bonjour,—supplies us with a new and pleasing theory of the unity of the poem. Chambers' tribute is well deserved: "Towards the study of *Beowulf* as a work of art, Professor Tolkien has made a contribution of the utmost importance." Whether or not we accept Tolkien's symbolism, he is certainly right with respect to the structure; and matters which he may have regarded as "points of minor tactics" clearly indicate that the poet was aware of the problems of unity posed by his balanced structure, and elaborated a carefully considered and effective design for the whole.

The poem seems to break in two only if we think of it exclusively in terms of its main action. At the end of Part I we leave the hero in his uncle Hygelac's court, a young champion who has done glorious deeds in Denmark, and whose loyal love for Hygelac is warmly returned; at the beginning of Part II we find him an old man, about to crown his own fifty-year reign with a final heroic sacrifice. The breach of continuity is not adequately bridged—indeed, it is made all the more apparent—by the brevity and swiftness of the transitional passage (lines 2200–10a) at the beginning of Part II. Obviously, if he had wished, the poet might have gone far to bridge this gap: whether or not he had traditional basis for any exploits of his hero during the fifty-year reign, he surely knew—for in lines 2354–96 he tells us—of Beowulf's gallant stand in Frisia, his slaying of Dæghrefn and his escape, his refusal of the crown, his protection of the boy-king Heardred, and his expedition against Onela. This is God's plenty; and it is exactly the kind of stuff of which heroic lays were made. The poet could have made much of all this if he had wished; and he might easily have accounted for the long reign without revealed incident as the direct result of the power won by Beowulf in his alliance with Eadgils and through the defeat of Onela. Indeed, he seems to have conceived it so: for Beowulf, as he lies dying, asserts that 'there has not been a king of any neighboring people who has dared approach me with weapons' (lines 2733b–35).

If we compare the treatment, in *Grettissaga*, of the Icelandic outlaw's fight against the trolls of the waterfall with Beowulf's triumphs over Grendel and his dam, we see at once how capable our poet was of transforming into noble epic narrative the thinner stuff of folk-tale. How much more, then, might he have made of the hero's deeds in those middle years, from his valiant fight in Frisia through his magnanimous service to

Heardred, and his retaliation for Heardred's death! He preferred to present them in a summary of intervening action; and this must have been his deliberate choice.

What determined that choice was evidently his judgment as an artist—a sound judgment; for to have treated these intervening events at length would have been to destroy his calculated balance, the exemplification of the heroic ideal in its two contrasted and most meaningful stages—first and last—of his hero's life. We are forever indebted to Tolkien for his perception of this. The poet wisely elected to subordinate, but *not* to sacrifice, such record as tradition gave him of his hero's exploits in the wars of peoples, and to use as his major theme the victories over monsters too formidable for any other champion to encounter. Through these he has revealed to us the matchless young hero, wise and loyal, brave and strong, beyond the measure of other men; and on the other hand, the old man still mightiest, facing certain death with unshrinking fortitude to save his people from the fury of the dragon. The sacrificial and triumphant death of Beowulf derives its meaning from this contrast. Had the poet stuffed his story with Beowulf's conquests of mortal foes, the incomparable "opposition of ends and beginnings" would have been lost: we should have gained a kind of English *chanson de geste,* and lost the world's noblest *Heldenleben.*

The poet carefully reinforces and points his "opposition of ends and beginnings": at the end of each part he has summed up the character and the *ethos* of his hero as revealed in the preceding narrative. Beowulf's loyalty to his lord, readiness to help the distressed, and magnanimity are emphasized in the fifty-five lines with which Part I concludes; his matchless courage despite the weight of years, his generosity and kindness to his followers, his devotion to his people, and his desire to deserve the esteem of men are expressed in the comment of Wiglaf and the Messenger in Part II, and in the eulogy uttered by his bereaved retainers as they perform his funeral rites. Most appropriately, the author places in Beowulf's own mouth the just and modest appraisal of his life: 'I have ruled this people fifty winters; there has been no king among the neighboring nations who has dared approach me with weapons, to threaten me with terror. I have awaited my appointed destiny in my own homeland, have held my own well; I have not sought strife, nor sworn oaths unrighteously. For all this, though sick with mortal wounds, I can rejoice; for the Ruler of Men will have no cause to reproach me with murder of kin when my life departs from the body.' (Lines 2732–43a.)

Herein lies the only *advance:* in the first part of the poem Beowulf has been presented as the ideal retainer and champion; in the second, he is the ideal king. In his passage from the lesser role to the greater, his heroic virtues inevitably find larger, though similar, modes of expression. We do not see his temper change, or his character develop: we see them reveal themselves appropriately and consistently in every action and situation.

In a heroic poem so conceived and constructed as "an opposition of ends and beginnings," the person of the hero must provide the essential bond between the balanced parts. It is so in the *Iliad,* the structure of which is very different from that of *Beowulf:* it is the person of Achilles through which the inner unity is maintained. But the hero functions within a very complex action, which must not be allowed to escape his domination. Therefore Homer confines all the action within the period of the wrath and reconciliation of Achilles: the fortunes of all the Greeks and Trojans depend upon *his* action or inaction, so that we feel the portent of his spirit behind all that is said or done; all that occurs falls within the few days of the wrath and in the period immediately following its resolution. The fate of Troy lies in the heart of Achilles, and is decided with the death of Patroclus.

There is no such unity of time or place in the *Odyssey;* though here also the resourceful, indomitable hero makes himself continuously felt. The structure of the poem arises out of the person of the hero: all the sorrows and wanderings of Odysseus result from a single act of his—the blinding of Polyphemus; and the story is brought together as Odysseus himself tells his toils and buffetings to Alcinous and the Phaeacian court. The resolution comes as the direct consequence of this narration by the hero; and in that moment the poet makes his hero appear to Homer's audience at his greatest and most sympathetic, through the eyes of the Phaeacian audience of Odysseus himself.

The nature of the main action of *Beowulf*, split as it is by a time-gap of more than fifty years, confronted its poet with a problem more difficult than Homer had to face. Beowulf's return home after his victories in Denmark, and the beautiful scene at the Geatish court, successfully avert a breach of the unity of place; but the very need to maintain a calculated balance compelled discontinuity of action. But it is only the main plot which suffers discontinuity; the action of the subplot is continuous, and is made, in all its parts, to pivot upon a single historical event. This event has the most decisive effect upon the hero's career, and upon the fates both of his people and of the Danes. It is through the poet's management of the death of Hygelac, and of Beowulf's relations to Hygelac, that the effect of discontinuity in the main action is overcome, and unity achieved.

—Arthur Gilchrist Brodeur, *The Art of* Beowulf (Berkeley:
University of California Press, 1959), pp. 72–75

## KENNETH SISAM ON CHRISTIANITY IN *BEOWULF*

[Kenneth Sisam (1887–1971) is the author of *Cynewulf and His Poetry* (1933), *Studies in the History of Old English Literature* (1953), and *The Structure of* Beowulf (1965), from which the following extract is taken. Here, Sisam explores the Christian references and themes in *Beowulf* and argues that Christianity was a secondary concern for the poet.]

If there were no other evidence than the Christian allusions, one could safely infer that *Beowulf* was earlier than the post-Conquest *Chanson de Roland*, where the heroes have benediction and absolution, and saints carry them to Paradise; or than the thirteenth-century *Nibelungenlied*, where the motives of the plot are savage, but Christian forms are a matter of course: Siegfried has a cathedral funeral, Gunther takes a chaplain with him on his journey, and, if tradition forbade making Attila a Christian, he practises religious tolerance, and mass may be celebrated at his court. These heroic poems belong to a later period of Western Christianity. But in England, where even nominal Christianity was not established in all kingdoms until the late seventh century, one would expect at that time, or in the eighth, or even the early ninth century, a gradation from near-paganism to the Christianity of Cuthbert, Bede, or Alcuin. The Christian allusions in *Beowulf* are of the kind that would be readily appreciated by the audience I have assumed, i.e. all the company assembled for entertainment in the hall of a great layman, among whom there would be more and less instructed, more and less devout.

Of course the poet knew much more of the Scriptures than he put into *Beowulf,* whether he learned it from preachers or from Christian poetry in the vernacular or from books. But how deep was his Christianity on the evidence of the text? Professor Tolkien supposed that he represented the Heroic Age to a Christian audience as pagan, noble, and hopeless, and that the hero himself is shown as essentially pagan. If by 'Christian' is meant one who accepts the teaching of the Gospels, then Beowulf is a noble pagan, whether or not his references to God, God's light, and Judgement can be explained away. But great difficulties stand in the way of all explanations that make the poet a deep thinker, attempting themes and ways of conveying them that might be tried on a select body of readers in a more advanced age. Hrothgar does not fit into the picture of a pagan age. 'He refers all things to the favour of God, and never omits thanks for mercies.' He does not express an unchristian thought. He is represented as noble but certainly not pagan.

I prefer a simpler explanation: that in this work the poet was not much concerned with Christianity and paganism. Beowulf was a hero mainly because of his deeds. All his adventures come from pagan stories, and the pagan motives and actions persist. Hrothgar is made eminent by his speeches, which were not governed by pagan tradition. The Christian poet was free to mould them as he wished, and so to make belief in God a leading feature of the character. He was likely to make the most of it, since Hrothgar is not just the pathetic figure of a king incapable through old age of protecting his people: he is a famous hero, still great because of his wisdom and goodness.

The same hand drew both characters and both are intended to be admired. There is no criticism of anything Beowulf says or does, however unchristian it may be. His doctrine of revenge, his eagerness for material rewards and earthly fame, his silence about a future life, all pass without comment. His satisfaction that God cannot blame him for the murder of kinsmen (2741f.) is paralleled in the poet's earlier praise: 'he did not slay his comrades in their cups' (2179f.). And it is worth noting that, if all Hrothgar's speeches are accepted as belonging to the original composition, they put forward no characteristically Christian doctrine. Most intelligent men would agree that overweening is a vice, especially in the crude forms that Hrothgar thinks of— miserliness, rapacity, and the wanton killing of companions (1709ff.). Reversals of fortune (1769ff.) are a commonplace subject of reflection and story among pagans. So are the shortness and uncertainty of human life (1753ff.): Homer had said more concisely that ten thousand ways of death lie close about us, and no man can flee or avoid them.

In short, there is little in *Beowulf* that is distinctively Christian in the strict sense. The words and conduct of the ideal characters are for the most part designed to show qualities such as courage, loyalty, generosity, and wisdom, which are admired by good men of any creed. Other characteristics, such as determination to exact vengeance, are not in accord with Christian doctrine, but were probably still admired by the majority of Anglo-Saxons in Christian times.

—Kenneth Sisam, *The Structure of* Beowulf (Oxford: Clarendon Press, 1965), pp. 76–79

[E. Talbot Donaldson (1910–1987), one of the most notable scholars of medieval literature in his time, taught at Yale, Columbia, and Indiana University, where he was Distinguished Professor of English. In this extract from the introduction to his prose translation of *Beowulf,* Donaldson explores the significance of tribalism and kinship in the poem.]

The relationship between kinsmen was also of deep significance to this society and provides another emotional value for Old English heroic poetry. If one of his kinsmen had been slain, a man had the special duty of either killing the slayer or exacting from him the payment of *wergild* ("man-price"): each rank of society was evaluated at a definite price, which had to be paid to the dead man's kinsmen by the killer who wished to avoid their vengeance—even if the killing had been accidental. Again, the money itself had less significance as wealth than as a proof that the kinsmen had done what was right. Relatives who failed either to exact *wergild* or to take vengeance could never be happy, having found no practical way of satisfying their grief for their kinsmen's death. "It is better for a man to avenge his friend than much mourn," Beowulf says to the old Hrothgar, who is bewailing Aeschere's killing by Grendel's mother. And one of the most poignant passages in the poem describes the sorrow of King Hrethel after one of his sons had accidentally killed another: by the code of kinship Hrethel was forbidden to kill or to exact compensation from a kinsman, yet by the same code he was required to do one or the other in order to avenge the dead. Caught in this curious dilemma, Hrethel became so disconsolate that he could no longer face life.

It is evident that the need to take vengeance would create never-ending feuds, which the practice of marrying royal princesses to the kings or princes of hostile tribes did little to mitigate, though the purpose of such marriages was to replace hostility by alliance. Hrothgar wishes to make peace with the Heatho-Bards by marrying his daughter to their king, Ingeld, whose father was killed by the Danes; but as Beowulf predicts, sooner or later the Heatho-Bards' desire for vengeance on the Danes will erupt, and there will be more bloodshed. And the

Danish princess Hildeburh, married to Finn of the Jutes, will see her son and her brother both killed while fighting on opposite sides in a battle at her own home, and ultimately will see her husband killed by the Danes in revenge for her brother's death. Beowulf himself is, for a Germanic hero, curiously free of involvement in feuds of this sort, though he does boast that he avenged the death of his king, Heardred, on his slayer Onela. Yet the potentiality—or inevitability—of sudden attack, sudden change, swift death is omnipresent in *Beowulf:* men seem to be caught in a vast web of reprisals and counterreprisals from which there is little hope of escape. This is the aspect of the poem which is apt to make the most powerful impression on the reader—its strong sense of doom.

Beowulf himself is chiefly concerned not with tribal feuds but with fatal evil both less and more complex. Grendel and the dragon are threats to the security of the lands they infest just as human enemies would be, but they are not part of the social order and presumably have no one to avenge their deaths (that Grendel's mother appeared as an avenger seems to have been a surprise both to Beowulf and to the Danes). On the other hand, because they are outside the normal order of things, they require of their conqueror something greater than normal warfare requires. In each case, it is the clear duty of the king and his companions to put down the evil. But the Danish Hrothgar is old and his companions unenterprising, and excellent though Hrothgar has been in the kingship, he nevertheless lacks the quality that later impels the old Beowulf to fight the dragon that threatens his people. The poem makes no criticism of Hrothgar for this lack; he merely seems not to be the kind of man—one might almost say he was not fated—to develop his human potential to the fullest extent that Fate would permit: that is Beowulf's role. In undertaking to slay Grendel, and later Grendel's mother, Beowulf is testing his relationship with unknowable destiny. At any time, as he is fully aware, his luck may abandon him and he may be killed, as, indeed, he is in the otherwise successful encounter with the dragon. But whether he lives or dies, he will have done all that any man could do to develop his character heroically. It is this consciousness of testing Fate that probably explains the boasting that modern readers of heroic poetry often find offensive. When he boasts,

Beowulf is not only demonstrating that he has chosen the heroic way of life, but is also choosing it, for when he invokes his former courage as pledge of his future courage, his boast becomes a vow; the hero has put himself in a position from which he cannot withdraw.

—E. Talbot Donaldson, "The Poem," *Beowulf,* tr. E. Talbot Donaldson (New York: Norton, 1966), pp. x–xi

## EDWARD B. IRVING, JR. ON WIGLAF

[Edward B. Irving, Jr. (b. 1923), formerly a professor of English at the University of Pennsylvania, is the author of *A Reading of* Beowulf (1968) and *Rereading* Beowulf (1989). In this extract, Irving examines the character of Wiglaf and his relationship with Beowulf.]

In a way it may seem as though Beowulf's own past, his own youth, takes form and joins him here in the person of Wiglaf, but Wiglaf has more to do with the future than with the past. He represents continuity in time, for by his own free act in response to Beowulf's danger he takes on the great heritage of human responsibility. At this present moment, that responsibility is expressed in the form of collaboration, as the two men take their stand to meet a second onslaught from the dragon. When Wiglaf's wooden shield is consumed by fire, he must take shelter behind his king's shield. As he does this, Beowulf, perhaps in an attempt to cover his retreat, strikes another blow at the dragon, this time delivered so powerfully that his great sword Nægling is shattered. Immediately the dragon makes its third rush and its sharp poisoned teeth close around Beowulf's neck.

"Then," cries the poet triumphantly, "I heard that in the time of need the warrior who stood beside the mighty king made his courage known, and his strength and his bravery, as it was a part of him from birth!" Wiglaf, his hand burned by the fire, moves forward to stab the dragon in a vital spot "a little farther down." And the wounded Beowulf recovers himself enough to use his dagger to cut through the dragon's body. "They killed the enemy, both those noble kinsmen destroyed him," exults the poet, using the plural very pointedly. For it is the loving and self-sacrificing relationship between the two men that itself seems to gain the final victory over the monster, and the ensuing lines which tell of the last moments of Beowulf's life continue to lay great stress on the intimate bond connecting this society of two. Wiglaf laves the wounded Beowulf with water, and then hurries to bring the treasures from the barrow so that Beowulf may look at them before he dies. As he looks at the great strength of the well-built "eternal earth house," Beowulf is thinking of death, and he regrets that he has no son of his own to leave the dragon hoard to, but then he bequeaths the treasure together with the responsibility for the kingdom to Wiglaf. Just as Beowulf himself once became the adopted son of old Hrothgar for a time, now Wiglaf seems to have earned by his courage and devotion something like the title of son to Beowulf. The dying king's last gesture is both ritualistic and intimate: he gives his gold neck ring and his weapons to the young warrior, and "told him to use them well." And his last words are addressed to Wiglaf: "You are the last survivor of our race, the Wægmundings. *Wyrd* [fate] has swept away all my kinsmen to their destiny, warriors in their courage; I must now follow them." (2813–16) ⟨. . .⟩

When Beowulf dies, the poet tells us, in unmistakably Christian terms, that "his soul went out of his breast to go seek the judgment and glory of the just" (2819–20). If we were reading an Anglo-Saxon poem about the life of a saint, we would find that a statement like this would usually be the starting point for an elaborate final development of the theme of the triumphant journey homeward into the joy and security of the other world (Christian poets were not averse to representing it as a return from exile into the Great Mead Hall of God's heroes). But in *Beowulf* this brief remark is almost all we have to suggest the existence of an afterlife as Christians know it. Instead of enlarging on this subject at this point, the poet adds a rather curious meditation on the tableau now formed by the lifeless bodies of Beowulf and the dragon, lying side by side. He lays special stress on the dragon's motionlessness: it lies still now on the earth, where once it used to range exuberantly in playful flights at midnight. In part this passage belongs to the traditional pattern in heroic poetry of the triumph over a fallen enemy, but the more the dragon is dwelt on, the more conscious we become of Beowulf's own immobility. The desperate Wiglaf continues to try to revive his king with water, but this repeated action has no other effect than to remind us that Wiglaf cannot make his king move again. In the intensely physical world of epic poetry, death is, above all else, to be strengthless and inert.

—Edward B. Irving, Jr., *Introduction to* Beowulf (Englewood Cliffs, NJ: Prentice-Hall, 1969), pp. 84–85, 88–89

## MARTIN PUHVEL ON *BEOWULF* AND IRISH FOLKLORE

[Martin Puhvel (b. 1933) is a professor of English at McGill University in Montreal. He is the author of Beowulf *and Celtic Tradition* (1979), from which the following extract is taken. Here, Puhvel argues for a connection between *Beowulf* and Irish folklore in the episode of the melting of the giant-made sword.]

The melting, through the hot, poisonous blood of Grendel's Mother (or, conceivably, Grendel) of the mighty giant-made sword which Beowulf finds in the subaquatic "hall" and with which he slays the ogress and decapitates her dead son, is an element to which no clear-cut parallel is found in recorded Germanic tradition. The only instance of some degree of resemblance is met in a nineteenth-century Icelandic folktale, which tells of a farm-labourer's obtaining a fairy scythe which operates by itself, even with several blades attached. The man is told by the fairy donor never to hold it over fire (while whetting it). One day his wife lends it to a neighbour, in whose keeping it will, however, not mow. Ignoring the warning of the wife, the borrower tries to whet it over fire; as soon as the blade is touched by the flame, it melts like wax and only a lump of metal remains.

The resemblance of this element to the melting of the sword in *Beowulf* is, clearly, of a superficial nature. The kernel of the story is the mutability under certain conditions, often at the breaking of a taboo, of fairy-endowed objects; hyper-destructive blood or extremes of heat and venom play no role here.

Significant parallels are, on the other hand, found in Irish tradition. Thus in a modern Irish folktale Finn mac Cumaill places the head of the slain Curucha na Gras on top of a holly bush; "the minute he put it there the head burnt the bush to the earth, and the earth to the clay."

⟨. . .⟩ What matters is that we do have evidence of an Irish tradition of fantastically hot or otherwise destructive blood, whether it sets a bush aflame, makes water boil or snow melt, consumes solid rock, scathes warriors' spears, or dissolves a human being. As the motif of hyper-destructive blood is, aside from *Beowulf,* not recorded in Germanic areas, there exists a very considerable likelihood that the element of the melting of the giant-wrought sword in *Beowulf* is indebted to Irish tradition.

—Martin Puhvel, Beowulf *and Celtic Tradition* (Waterloo, Ontario: Wilfrid Laurier University Press, 1979), pp. 40, 43–44

JOHN D. NILES ON THE ROLE OF THE NARRATOR IN *BEOWULF*

[John D. Niles (b. 1945) is a professor of English at the University of California at Berkeley and the author of *Old English Literature in Context* (1980) and Beowulf: *The Poem and Its Tradition* (1983), from which the following extract is taken. Here, Niles explores the nature of the first-person narrator in *Beowulf.*]

The chief function of the narrator's voice is to validate the story and comment on it—to "authenticate" it for the listeners. The habitual stance of the narrator has been aptly described as one of "authority based on exceptional knowledge about a common tradition."

From the poem's first lines, the narrator suppresses his individuality to present himself as one of the group, the other members of which constitute the listening audience. "Lo, we have heard," he begins, shunning the personal voice of the Anglo-Saxon elegies. The narrator claims to speak only what is common knowledge.

Eventually this first-person plural voice merges almost unnoticeably into the first-person singular. After the first line, as the story becomes more specific, the narrator never again uses the pronoun *we* in relation to his knowledge of his sources. A bare dozen times (in lines 38, 62, 74, 1011, 1027, 1196, 1197, 1842, 2163, 2172, 2694, and 2773) he uses the pronoun *I* in phrases of the sort "I have heard that"; or "I have heard, then . . ."; or, in comparative constructions, "I have not heard of" (a more comely ship, or more generous king, and so forth). Another five times (in lines 776, 837, 1955, 2685, and 2837) he uses the fixed formula "by my account" or, perhaps, "according to my version of the story." None of these phrases is meant to call up the idea of a human being with an individual sensibility or with an original story to relate. At the most, they suggest that the narrator speaks from his deep familiarity with the stories of Germanic antiquity, a familiarity that he has gained from oral tradition. Many stories of old times are told, the narrator suggests. Of these he has chosen one for retelling.

Apart from these few instances of first-person asides, *Beowulf* may seem to be a story that tells itself. Its immediate impression on a reader is likely to be that of direct, unmediated narrative, much like that of *Genesis A* or *Exodus.* The falsity of this impression becomes evident as soon as one considers how frequently the narrator uses gnomic statements, superlatives, and explicit ethical judgments to build up a grid of belief against which the action he recounts can be plotted. The narrator is not with us only intermittently, at moments when he speaks of his having heard the story; he is a constant presence throughout. His one great function is to put his listeners into the position of his ideal audience, an audience that nods assent to all his judgments. Because these judgments are not the property of any one person but have been handed down as collective wisdom, the narrator does not really manipulate his audience, as an author of propaganda might. One could think of the poem as a process whereby a society's traditional system of values or beliefs is articulated so that it can be appreciated more deeply by all those present.

The narrator in *Beowulf* is not omniscient, though he has been called that. He speaks what he knows of the actors in the story, much as Hrothgar's thane recounts "just about all that he had heard said concerning Sigemund's courageous deeds" (874b–876a). Usually he observes a respectful silence concerning things that no mortal could be expected to know. "People know not how to say truly" who received Scyld's funeral boat (50b–51a), just as "no one knows" the movements of the secret creatures of hell (162b–163). These matters he accepts as mysteries. On the other hand, his knowledge of Beowulf's adventures seems to have no limits, for he is able to describe, for example, the hero's fortunes even at the bottom of Grendel's mere. At one point he moves back in time to recount the words of a speaker who died hundreds of years before this story begins (2247–66). He knows of Grendel's descent from Cain, even though there is no indication that the people in the narrative do, and he knows that Beowulf's soul is saved, even though the Geats do not. To call him "near-omniscient" hits close to the mark. Although like many a storyteller he sometimes claims knowledge that no one could really possess, he more often plays the role of an informal historian who repeats what he has heard from common report.
    —John D. Niles, Beowulf: *The Poem and Its Tradition* (Cambridge, MA: Harvard University Press, 1983), pp. 198–200

RICHARD BUTTS ON GRENDEL'S MERE

[Richard Butts teaches at the University of Toronto. In this extract, Butts discusses the poet's challenge of conveying a suitable sense of terror in describing Grendel's mere.]

The technical challenge which the *Beowulf* poet must overcome in relation to the mere is the inadequacy of language to convey a complex and subtle state of mind, in this case, the psychological mood of men toward Grendel and all the greater unknown which he represents. The principal difficulty encountered in describing a psychological mood is that it resists most forms of univocal description. The linguistic problem points to a deeper epistemological one. Hrothgar tells Beowulf: 'No þæs frod leofaþ/gumena bearna, þæt þone grund wite' (1366b–1367b). The Dane's reference to the bottom of Grendel's mere is as much a figurative emblem of the limits of what can be known and said by men as it is an allusion to the depth of a body of water. Rendering a psychological mood poses a similar problem of description for the poet insofar as a state of mind or psychological mood is not as readily an object of sense as is, say, a 'sincfæt' or a 'guþsweord geatolic'. When the mind is turned inward to focus on a psychological mood as an object of knowledge, the mind must perceive it more intimately and less through the medium of sense; the process is more intuitive than it is empirical. Yet in spite of this rather formidable obstacle to communication, the poet does succeed in offering to his readers an understanding of a dominant psychological mood which is simply too exquisite to be contained within the conventional conceptual dimension of language. He communicates this mood through an analogical mode of thinking and description in which details of the physical landscape are consciously manipulated to evoke a psychological landscape.

Hrothgar calls the land in which Grendel and his mother live the 'dygel lond' (1357b). The dominant chord struck by the landscape description is one of otherworldliness, an intimation of the supernatural conveyed by the threatening images of the

> [. . .] wulfhleoþu, windige næssas,
> frecne fengelad, þær fyrgenstream
> under næssa genipu niþer gewiteþ,
> flod under foldan. (1358a–1361a)

The image of the 'wulfhleoþu' mediates between the natural and supernatural resonances of the landscape. Wolves do move in the natural landscape with which Hrothgar and Beowulf would be familiar, but these animals are also traditionally associated with death and the horrors of the battlefield where warriors pass from the world they know to the unknown beyond. The disappearance of the 'flod under foldan', with the 'fyrgenstream' flowing under the darkness of the headlands—foreshadowing Beowulf's descent into the water to do battle with Grendel's mother—is also emblematic on a more general level of this passage from light and the natural world to the mysterious darkness of whatever lies beyond it. The supernatural character of Grendel's mere is enhanced by the 'hrinde bearwas,/wudu wyrtum fæst' (1363a–1364b) which overshadow the water and the eerie spectacle which may be seen there each night, the 'niþwundor' (1365b) of the 'fyr on flode' (1366a). Perhaps the most powerful evocation of the supernatural, almost magical mood associated with Grendel's mere comes at the climax of Hrothgar's speech where the old king, in his attempt to impress upon Beowulf the very fearful and unnatural aspect of the place, tells the young Geat the story of the 'heorot hornum trum' (1369a), the extraordinary hart which gives up its life to the hounds rather than brave Grendel's mere.

—Richard Butts, "The Analogical Mere: Landscape and Terror in *Beowulf*," *English Studies* 68, No. 2 (1987): 114–15

## Mary A. Parker on Christianity and Language in *Beowulf*

[Mary A. Parker (b. 1946) has written *The Problem of Christianity and Secularism in* Beowulf (1984) and Beowulf *and Christianity* (1987), from which the following extract is taken. Here, Parker asserts that there is no dichotomy between the philosophy of the characters and the narrator of the poem.]

Comparative studies of word use and meaning complement the emerging picture of Anglo-Saxon society. Through an examination of the words of Hrothgar, Beowulf, and the poet-narrator, Chapter 4 evaluates the validity of Tolkien's suggestion that they are differentiated in philosophy and religious sentiments. Comparisons of content and language quickly reveal that all three voices advocate the same philosophy: they define success as victory in battle and expect fitting reward in the form of treasure; they agree that the duty of the king is to build a strong *comitatus* and to provide generous rewards for courage.

A comparison of expressions of Christian or religious sentiments reveals a similar convergence of views. Brodeur was right to reject Tolkien's distinction between Hrothgar, the "wise monotheist," and Beowulf, the noble pagan. They both refer to a god or a ruler in the same words about the same number of times. Both see death as "taking away" those whose time has come, and neither makes any reference to Christian doctrine. Hrothgar's admonition to Beowulf, which has been seen as referring to three of the seven deadly sins, is a formal speech expected by the retainers in the meadhall as the appropriate cautionary statement from the old king to an extremely successful warrior who can look forward to responsibilities of kingship himself one day. Hrothgar's subject is kingship, not pride, though he twice mentions pride (1740, 1760); nothing in Beowulf's behavior warrants reproof for excessive pride, except what the poet-narrator himself says (2345) about Beowulf's scorn for prudent battle tactics.

In addition to acknowledging the similarity of the characters' religious sentiments, we can now deny the distinction between the narrator and his characters. Robinson also saw no overt distinction between poet and characters, because he took the poet's purpose to be to hold in apposition both Christian and pagan worlds in order to create sympathy in the Anglo-Saxon audience for its doomed ancestors.

The poet's references to a god, though more numerous, are of the same type and are expressed in the same words as his characters use. He is as concerned with fate as Beowulf, and like the hero he sees it in a more superstitious than religious sense. The poet's vague references to "elsewhere" and the contrast of *wel* and *wa* (ll. 183–188) may be taken to concern heaven and hell, but they are not characterized clearly nor is there any doctrine given for earning either. The use of three stories from Genesis shows the points of immediate contact between the heroic society and Christianity. Cain is the exemplar of the man who kills his kinsmen, a concern of the secular society depicted in *Beowulf*. The circumstances of the story make the creation song appropriate, connecting the adorning of Heorot with the creation of the world. And the flood helps to explain the presence of giants, a common superstition reflected in other Old English literature.

The poet's reaction to the problem of Danish idol-worship and his use of pagan burial rites no longer need characterize him as a moralizing Christian who writes about a heathen past from a great remove in time and philosophy. The apostasy of the Danes does not show that the poet scorns the paganism of his characters as much as it shows a reality of Anglo-Saxon society as depicted by Bede; the last apostasy he recorded was among the East Saxons during the plague year 664. A charter also refers to apostasy among the Mercians c. 675. As seventh-century archaeological evidence for cremation and ship burial has demonstrated, the presence of pagan burial rites in the poem does not prove that the poet was representing ancient rituals. The fact that the details of these non-Christian burial practices in *Beowulf* do not match those in Viking accounts, because they omit human and animal sacrifice, does not show the poet producing a confused version of a pagan rite of which he had no direct knowledge. In fact, archaeological evidence shows that non-Christian and Christian burial practices existed together until the late seventh century and that there was a return to barrow burial in the same period. Also, all three ship burials found so far in England are from the first quarter of the seventh century and show signs of compromise with Christianity. None of these burials involves human sacrifice, and the great ship burial at Sutton Hoo contains what may be Christian symbols, especially the two silver baptismal spoons; of course, we have no way of knowing how these objects came to Sutton Hoo—perhaps as booty.

A new argument for unity may be made for *Beowulf* on the grounds that it reflects a reality about society at the time it was composed. As a poetic artifact of the culture that produced it, the poem reflects at least the idealized goals of the culture, if not the actual goals of living men. If *Beowulf* was written between 597 and 800, then it contributes to a study of the changes that Christianity brought to Anglo-Saxon life because it depicts the goals of that society at the crucial period of conversion. And if it reflects the effects of conversion on traditional poetic themes and language, the poem fits well into the picture of that society which can be drawn from other sources like history and archaeology.

This integration of various kinds of evidence provides a background against which to measure the conflicting opinions that commentators have expressed and probably will continue to express on the problem. The clearer the picture we draw of life in Anglo-Saxon England following the coming of Christianity, the better we can understand and appreciate the multi-layered society depicted in *Beowulf*.

The problem of Christianity in *Beowulf* is not best seen as a dichotomy between a pagan poem inexpertly covered with a veneer of Christianity and a sophisticated Christian allegory which makes use of traditional materials to teach a Christian lesson. It is more productive to accept *Beowulf* at face value, as an heroic poem of secular intent which contains pervasive Christian sentiments. It is not a pagan poem because "pagan" cannot be defined. It is not a pre-Christian poem because it contains strong Christian elements in its monotheism, its use of biblical materials, and perhaps its expression of "softened sentiments," though these may be attributable to an heroic code of behavior. The poem is not a Christian allegory because it makes no mention of allegorical or Christian purpose. It does moralize on secular matters, especially the role of the king, but Christianity has little or no overt part in the moral stance of the poem.

If we accept this combination of Christian and secular elements in *Beowulf*, then the poem can be seen as capturing a reality that we also see reflected in the history and archaeology of the period, a stage in the process of absorption of Christian culture in England. However, the stage is very long, and it is not easy to describe. I have limited my inquiry to the two-hundred year period from 597 to 800, but the increasingly well-known argument of Kevin Kiernan has indicated a date as late as the early eleventh century, increasing the span to four hundred years. Describing the stage of the Christianity in

*Beowulf* is a complex matter, to be pursued by studying both
Christian and secular aspects of Anglo-Saxon society.
—Mary A. Parker, Beowulf *and Christianity* (New York: Peter
Lang, 1987), pp. 199–201

FIDEL FAJARDO-ACOSTA ON THE BATTLE WITH GRENDEL'S
MOTHER

[Fidel Fajardo-Acosta is the author of *The
Condemnation of Heroism in the Tragedy of* Beowulf
(1989), from which the following extract is taken. Here,
Fajardo-Acosta studies the episode of Beowulf's battle
with Grendel's mother, which, he maintains, far from
being a triumphant rebirth, represents the true horror
of the epic—Beowulf's transformation into a monster.]

Structural studies of *Beowulf* cannot fail to identify the battle
with Grendel's mother as the central episode of the story. Niles
and others have convincingly demonstrated that the *Beowulf*
poet's technique of composition is characterized by the use of
ring or envelope patterns. Niles interprets these structures as a
means of obliquely approaching particularly gruesome subject
matter: "ring composition enables the poet to ease into and
out of a picture of past terrors." The overall structure of the
poem suggests that the battle with Grendel's mother is the
central horror and climax of the story:

> . . . many of these correspondences, both great and small, con-
> verge on a single narrative event of great intensity: the hero's
> struggle against Grendel's dam in the depths of the monster's
> pool. The choice of this event as the structural center of the epic
> is not casual. It is at this point in the narrative that the young
> hero Beowulf has his closest brush with death.

The centrality of the episode seems to be both structural and
thematic. The events in the mere-cave mark a transformation in
Beowulf himself which will have a great impact on his future
and that of his people. Although she fails to perceive the

dreadful nature of the change that Beowulf undergoes in the mere, Vaught correctly notes that the adventure is "the moment in the poem when he attains his selfhood." This selfhood is, unfortunately, the monster self that will bring about the destruction of Beowulf and the Geats. The obscurity that surrounds the adventure, characterized by Niles as "the point of greatest mystery," hides events which are shameful and unspeakable. As Nicholson suggests, Beowulf "tells Hygelac about his fight with Grendel's mother, but glosses over certain details that might seem shameful."

Beowulf's experiences in the mere belong to the category of what Arnold van Gennep calls "rites of passage," that is, "ceremonies whose essential purpose is to enable the individual to pass from one defined position to another which is equally well defined." It is entirely justified to consider the adventure as a sort of initiation and "symbolic death." Quoting Hubert and Mauss, van Gennep points out that "the idea of a momentary death is a general theme of magical as well as religious initiation." The battle with Grendel's mother represents the initiation of Beowulf into full-fledged Cain-gianthood, and into the status of demonic being. At the same time, his former self, his gentle humanity, suffers an irrevocable blow which effectively constitutes the death of Beowulf the man at the hands of Beowulf the monster. Exploring the significance of Aeneas' descent into the underworld, Bodkin remarks that "Virgil's account of the descent to Hades is determined, largely or in part, by his knowledge of the initiation Mysteries." She agrees with Fowler in believing that "the character of Aeneas is shown as changed by his underworld journey." The suggestions that Beowulf's return from the mere-lake represents a form of symbolic rebirth is a notion which can only be justified if "rebirth" is understood as the birth of the monster. Comparisons of Beowulf's rebirth with Christ's resurrection are, however, grossly inappropriate. Christ's resurrection constitutes the rebirth of the very spirit of gentleness which Beowulf loses and leaves behind buried in the depths of the mere-cave.

—Fidel Fajardo-Acosta, *The Condemnation of Heroism in the Tragedy of* Beowulf (Lewiston, NY: Edwin Mellen Press, 1989), pp. 83–84

[Christine Alfano was, at the time she wrote this paper, a doctoral candidate in English at Stanford University. In this extract, Alfano argues that the "monstrosity" of Grendel's mother is largely a product of readers' acceptance of misogynist beliefs regarding the proper role of women.]

One might expect that the feminist movement would have liberated Grendel's mother from her marginalization. Even Edward Irving credits contemporary feminism for his revised approach to *Beowulf,* and specifically to Grendel's mother:

> That [Grendel's mother] is extraordinarily embedded in her natural (or unnatural) surroundings in the evil mere was clear to me when I wrote *A Reading of Beowulf.* But it now seems remarkable that my own unconscious biases then prevented me from perceiving an even more significant way of embedding someone in a stereotype. She is, once you notice it, systematically reduced, ignored, discredited, and deprived of the ordinary dignity any ravening monster is entitled to—because of her sex. It is important to acknowledge that the feminist movement has given us the power to open our eyes to this kind of embedding.

There are still, however, "unconscious biases" at work. She is, for Irving, still monstrous. Although "the feminist movement" has opened Irving's eyes to her marginalization, it has not compelled him to question it. Herein lies what I believe may be the paradox of this problem of monstrosity. It is possible that the feminist criticism of the past fifteen years has perpetuated, legitimized, and even institutionalized the idea of Grendel's mother as monster. As a result of Nina Auerbach's, Sandra Gilbert's, and Susan Gubar's work, the angel-monster dichotomy is now a commonplace in interpreting images of powerful women in literature. In fact, I believe that it is due to the success of their theories and others like them that this "woman-as-monster" trope has achieved almost archetypal status. As with any archetype, however, the chief danger then lies in its complacent acceptance. The critic or reader searches for, finds, and analyzes the archetype; but never thinks to question how, or whether, it actually came to be embedded in the text. Consequently, while such scholars believe that they are finding the epitome of "feminine monstrosity" in Grendel's mother, they are possibly simply reading this image into *Beowulf.*

This is evident when examining the way Gilbert and Gubar discuss the "monster" trope in *The Madwoman in the Attic.* Although in some instances they cite actual female monsters in literature, such as Spenser's Errour, Milton's Sin, and Swift's "Goddess Criticism," the majority of their examples illustrate figurative monstrosity. When discussing Shakespeare's Lady Macbeth, Goneril, and Regan, or the mother of Elizabeth Barrett Browning's Aurora Leigh, or Charlotte Brontë's Bertha, Gilbert and Gubar do not interpret these women as subhuman creatures. Their arguments instead focus on the monstrous imagery surrounding these characters, which separates them from their angelic counterparts. In many ways, Jane Chance situates her article in this tradition of categorizing feminine types; however, as do most scholars who discuss Grendel's mother, she too readily reads "monstrous imagery" as "monstrosity" and therefore categorizes the unconventional woman as monster.

One reason this slippage is so inevitable is that Gilbert, Gubar, and Auerbach deal primarily with untranslated texts. When there is an intermediary between narrative and reader, their theories are not so readily applicable. Before we can make any valid analyses, we must distinguish between the original text and the text reconfigured by secondary sources and critical tools. It is also significant that Gilbert, Gubar, and Auerbach all contend that the woman-as-monster stereotype flourished principally during the nineteenth century. Since that century hosted the first major surge of Anglo-Saxon scholarship, the first Old English scholars were probably at least partially responsible for incorporating feminine monster imagery into the *Beowulf* text. Grendel's mother might possess some attributes of what Gilbert and Gubar define as "monstrosity:" her character and actions defy traditional gender assumptions. However, this monstrous imagery does not lie in physical claws or in talons, but rather in her alienation, her ties to the Cain-kin, and her defiance of traditional gender conventions. In fact, a large part of her reputed monstrosity lies not in Grendel's mother, but in Grendel himself. Lacking any identity independent of her son's even in name, Grendel's mother replicates the historical experience of millions of women who were defined through their male relatives. She finds herself implicated in her child's monstrosity, as unchallenged assumptions subsume her maternal role within a son's identity. Refusing to differentiate between mother and son, these translators, lexicographers, and critics transform her into a inhuman beast; and readers consume their modified texts as if they represent authoritative truth. The process is simple and self-complementing; nevertheless, it is also unjustified. The reader must resist and challenge this tradition, so as to liberate the translated work from its critical baggage. It is time to relieve Grendel's mother from her burden of monstrosity and reinstate her in her deserved position as *ides, aglœcwif:* "lady, warrior-woman."

—Christine Alfano, "The Issue of Feminine Monstrosity: A<br>Revaluation of Grendel's Mother," Comitatus 23 (1992): 10–12

## JAMES W. EARL ON THE DIFFICULTIES OF *BEOWULF*

[James W. Earl is a professor of English at the University of Oregon. In this extract from his book on *Beowulf,* Earl explores some of the difficulties of the poem for students and scholars alike.]

*Beowulf* has a bad reputation: Woody Allen advises English majors, "Just don't take any course where they make you read *Beowulf.*" Despite its foreignness and its difficulty, however, and despite its funereal obsession with death, *Beowulf* is now commonly taught to ninth graders, along with the *Iliad* and the *Odyssey,* as if it were an adventure or fantasy story. This trivialization accounts for some of the poem's bad reputation, but not all of it.

*Beowulf* is a hard text. Its language, style, and values seem as distant and strange as those of Homer and the Greek tragedies. Like them, *Beowulf* opens up a metrical world parallel to our own, different but strangely akin, throwing our ideas and attitudes, some of them unconscious, into new light. But our kinship with the world of *Beowulf*—our perspective in this new light—always remains hauntingly out of focus. Today a good reader of *Beowulf* has to be an expert time traveler and mystery unraveler—an expert scholar and interpreter; but even so, it remains uncertain what we can learn from the poem that is not wholly contingent on our own attitudes and beliefs. It is not at all clear that a "clean" interpretation is possible. This may be true of all texts to a degree, but again, *Beowulf* is an extreme case.

The poet and his first readers already had something of the same problem, however. The world of *Beowulf,* set in the heroic past, was already distant from them, akin to but strangely different from their Christian Anglo-Saxon world. Between the world of the poem and the world of its poet lay not only the gulf of meter but the complex transformations, social and psychological, of the development from tribe to state and of the conversion to Christianity. The relation of the Germanic tribal elements in the poem to Christianity has always been its most notorious crux and the driving force of its criticism. *Beowulf* is an ethical poem of the Christian Anglo-Saxons, but its ethics are not Christian, and its hero is not an Anglo-Saxon; so it is not clear how the poem's ideals might actually have functioned in the actual world of the audience.

Many scholars meditating on this problem have concluded that an Anglo-Saxon audience could not have accepted the poem's non-Christian ("pagan") ideals, so it is commonly argued that the poem's heroic warrior virtues are actually metaphors for Christian ones. Lately it is even commonly said that the poem's greatness may lie precisely in the way it subtly undermines those heroic ideals—in effect, undermines itself. Robert Hanning, for example, argues that the poet "completely reverses all tendencies toward harmony in heroic history, and offers instead a soured, ironic version of what has gone on before, embodying a final assessment of a world without God as a world in which time and history are themselves negative concepts." T. A. Shippey claims "that the poet is demonstrating the inadequacy of heroic society; that he sees this the more forcibly for being a Christian; and that his rejection of overt finger-pointing first gives the pleasure of ironic perception, and second shows the glittering insidiousness of heroism, the way it perverts even the best of intentions." The latest major statement of this position is Bernard Huppé's *Hero in the Earthly City*. These are modern readings of *Beowulf*. They are not entirely false, but they are unlikely simplifications, because they still leave many questions unasked.

A few questions I like to ask are these: (1) How do the psychologies of tribal and civilized societies differ? (2) What are the psychological dynamics of the transition from one to the other, and of religious conversion? (3) How and why do we idealize the past? and (4) How do we identify with and internalize a work of literature? In any case, we can assume from the start that *Beowulf* bore a complex, indirect, and non-mimetic relation to any historical reality, including the Anglo-Saxon *ethos* either before or after the conversion.
—James W. Earl, *Thinking about* Beowulf (Stanford: Stanford University Press, 1994), pp. 165–67

# Editions of
# *Beowulf*

**Anglo-Saxon text:**

*De Danorum Rebus Gestis Secul. III & IV: Poema Danicum Dialecto Anglo-Saxonica.* Ed. Grímur Jónsson Thorkelin. 1815.

*Beowulf.* Ed. Moritz Heine. 1863. 2 vols.

*Beowulf: A Heroic Poem of the Eighth Century.* Ed. Thomas Arnold. 1876 (with English translation).

*Beowulf and The Fight at Finnsburg.* Ed. James M. Garnett. 1882 (with English translation).

*Beówulf: An Anglo-Saxon Poem.* Ed. James A. Harrison and Robert Sharp. 1883.

*Beowulf.* Ed. A. J. Wyatt. 1894, 1920 (rev. R. W. Chambers).

*Beowulf.* Ed. Alfred Holder. 1895–96. 3 vols.

*Beowulf and The Fight at Finnsburg.* Ed. Friedrich Klaeber. 1922.

*Beowulf, with the Finnsburg Fragment.* Ed. C. L. Wrenn. 1953.

*Beowulf: Complete Text in Old English and Modern English.* Ed. E. Talbot Donaldson. 1967 (with English translation).

*Beowulf.* Ed. Robert D. Stevick. 1975.

*Beowulf: A Dual-Language Edition.* Ed. Howell D. Chickering, Jr. 1977 (with English translation).

*Beowulf.* Ed. Michael Swanton. 1978 (with English translation).

## English translations:

*A Translation of the Anglo-Saxon Poem of Beowulf.* Tr. John M. Kemble. 1837.

*The Deeds of Beowulf.* Tr. John Earle. 1892.

*Beowulf.* Tr. John Lesslie Hall. 1892.

*The Tale of Beowulf.* Tr. William Morris and A. J. Wyatt. 1895.

*Beowulf.* Tr. Chauncey Brewster Tinker. 1902.

*The Oldest English Epic.* Tr. Francis B. Gummere. 1909.

*Beowulf.* Tr. William Ellery Leonard. 1923.

*The Song of Beowulf.* Tr. R. K. Gordon. 1930.

*Beowulf, the Oldest English Epic.* Tr. Charles W. Kennedy. 1940.

*Beowulf.* Tr. David Wright. 1957.

*Beowulf.* Tr. Burton Raffel. 1963.

*Beowulf.* Tr. Lucien Dean Pearson. 1965.

*Beowulf.* Tr. E. Talbot Donaldson. 1966.

*Beowulf.* Tr. Kevin Crossley-Holland. 1968.

*Beowulf and Its Analogues.* Tr. G. N. Garmonsway and Jacqueline Simpson, 1968.

*Beowulf.* Tr. Marijane Osborn. 1983.

*Beowulf.* Tr. Ruth P. M. Lehmann. 1988.

*Beowulf: A Translation and Commentary.* Tr. Marc Hudson. 1990.

*Beowulf.* Tr. Barry Tharaud. 1990.

# Works about
# *Beowulf*

Abraham, Lenore. "The Decorum of Beowulf." *Philological Quarterly* 72 (1993): 267–87.

Anderson, George K. *The Literature of the Anglo-Saxons.* 2nd ed. Princeton: Princeton University Press, 1966.

Benson, Larry D. "The Originality of *Beowulf.*" *Harvard English Studies* 1 (1970): 1–43.

Berger, Harry, Jr., and H. Marshall Leicester, Jr. "Social Structure as Doom: The Limits of Heroism in *Beowulf.*" In *Old English Studies in Honour of John C. Pope,* ed. Robert B. Burlin and Edward B. Irving, Jr. Toronto: University of Toronto Press, 1974, pp. 37–79.

Bloom, Harold, ed. *Beowulf.* New York: Chelsea House, 1987.

Bolton, Whitney F. *Alcuin and* Beowulf: *An Eighth-Century View.* New Brunswick, NJ: Rutgers University Press, 1978.

Bonjour, Adrien. *Twelve* Beowulf *Papers.* Geneva: Droz, 1962.

Cable, Thomas W. *The Meter and Melody of* Beowulf. Urbana: University of Illinois Press, 1974.

Chadwick, Nora K. "The Monsters and Beowulf." In *The Anglo-Saxons,* ed. Peter Clemoes. London: Bowes, 1959, pp. 171–203.

Chase, Colin, ed. *The Dating of* Beowulf. Toronto: University of Toronto Press, 1981.

Chickering, Howell. "Lyric Time in *Beowulf.*" *Journal of English and Germanic Philology* 91 (1992): 489–509.

Clark, George. *Beowulf.* Boston: Twayne, 1990.

Cramp, Rosemary. "*Beowulf* and Archaeology." *Medieval Archaeology* 1 (1957): 57–77.

Creed, Robert Payson. *Reconstructing the Rhythm of* Beowulf. Columbia: University of Missouri Press, 1990.

Damico, Helen, and John Leyerle, ed. *Heroic Poetry in the Anglo-Saxon Period*. Kalamazoo: Western Michigan University, 1993.

Desmond, Marilynn. "*Beowulf:* The Monsters and the Tradition." *Oral Tradition* 7 (1992): 258–83.

Donahue, Charles. "*Beowulf* and Christian Tradition: A Reconsideration from a Celtic Stance." *Traditio* 21 (1965): 55–116.

Foley, John Miles, and J. Chris Womack, ed. *De Gustibus: Essays for Alain Renoir*. New York: Garland, 1992.

Fulk, R. D., ed. *Interpretations of* Beowulf: *A Critical Anthology*. Bloomington: Indiana University Press, 1991.

Gardner, John C. "*Beowulf.*" In Gardner's *The Construction of Christian Poetry in Old English*. Carbondale: Southern Illinois University Press, 1975, pp. 54–84.

Godfrey, Mary Flavia. "Beowulf and Judith: Thematizing Decapitation in Old English Poetry." *Texas Studies in Literature and Language* 35 (1993): 1–43.

Goldsmith, Margaret E. *The Mode and Meaning of* Beowulf. London: Athlone Press (University of London), 1970.

Greenfield, Stanley B. *Hero and Exile: The Art of Old English Poetry*. London: Hambledon Press, 1989.

Halverson, John. "The World of *Beowulf.*" *ELH* 36 (1969): 593–608.

Hanning, Robert W. "*Beowulf* as Heroic History." *Mediaevalia et Humanistica* 5 (1974): 77–102.

Harris, Joseph. "Beowulf's Last Words." *Speculum* 67 (1992): 1–32.

Hill, John M. *The Cultural World of* Beowulf. Toronto: University of Toronto Press, 1995.

Hume, Kathryn. "The Theme and Structure of *Beowulf.*" *Studies in Philology* 72 (1975): 1–27.

Huppe, Bernard Felix. *The Hero in the Earthly City: A Reading of* Beowulf. Binghamton, NY: Medieval & Renaissance Texts & Studies, 1984.

Irving, Edward B., Jr. *A Reading of* Beowulf. New Haven: Yale University Press, 1968.

———. *Rereading* Beowulf. Philadelphia: University of Pennsylvania Press, 1989.

John, Eric. "*Beowulf* and the Margins of Literacy." *Bulletin of the John Rylands Library* 56 (1974): 388–422.

Kendall, Calvin B. *The Metrical Grammar of* Beowulf. Cambridge: Cambridge University Press, 1991.

Kiernan, Kevin S. Beowulf *and the* Beowulf *Manuscript.* New Brunswick, NJ: Rutgers University Press, 1981.

McNamee, Maurice B. "Beowulf, a Christian Hero." In McNamee's *Honor and the Epic Hero*. New York: Henry Holt, 1960, pp. 86–117.

Mizuno, Tomoaki. "Beowulf as a Terrible Stranger." *Journal of Indo-European Studies* 17 (1989): 1–46.

Moorman, Charles. "The Essential Paganism of *Beowulf.*" *Modern Language Quarterly* 28 (1967): 3–18.

Morgan, Gwendolyn A. "Mothers, Monsters, Maturation: Female Evil in *Beowulf.*" *Journal of the Fantastic in the Arts* No. 13 (1991): 54–68.

Near, Michael R. "Anticipating Alienation: *Beowulf* and the Intrusion of Literacy." *PMLA* 108 (1993): 320–32.

Newton, Sam. *The Origins of* Beowulf *and the Pre-Viking Kingdom of East Anglia*. Cambridge: D. S. Brewer, 1993.

Nitzsche, Jane Chance. "The Structural Unity of *Beowulf*: The Problem of Grendel's Mother." *Texas Studies in Literature and Language* 22 (1980): 287–303.

Ogilvy, J. D. A., and Donald C. Baker. *Reading* Beowulf. Norman: University of Oklahoma Press, 1983.

Overling, Gillian R. *Language, Sign, and Gender in* Beowulf. Carbondale: Southern Illinois University Press, 1990.

Pearsall, Derek. "*Beowulf* and the Anglo-Saxon Poetic Tradition." In Pearsall's *Old English and Middle English Poetry*. London: Routledge & Kegan Paul, 1977, pp. 1–24.

Pope, John C. *The Rhythm of* Beowulf. New Haven: Yale University Press, 1966.

Robinson, Fred C. Beowulf *and the Appositive Style.* Knoxville: University of Tennessee Press, 1985.

———. *The Tomb of Beowulf and Other Essays on Old English.* Oxford: Basil Blackwell, 1993.

Schrader, Richard J. *Old English Poetry and the Genealogy of Events.* East Lansing, MI: Colleagues Press, 1993.

———. "Succession and Glory in *Beowulf.*" *Journal of English and Germanic Philology* 90 (1991): 491–504.

Sorrell, Paul. "Oral Poetry and the World of *Beowulf.*" *Oral Tradition* 7 (1992): 28–65.

Stitt, J. Michael. *Beowulf and the Bear's Son: Epic, Saga, and Fairytale in Northern Germanic Tradition.* New York: Garland, 1992.

Whitelock, Dorothy. *The Audience of* Beowulf. 2nd ed. Oxford: Clarendon Press, 1958.

Wormald, Patrick. "Bede, *Beowulf,* and the Conversion of the Anglo-Saxon Aristocracy." In *Bede and Anglo-Saxon England,* ed. Robert T. Farrell. Oxford: British Archaeological Reports, 1978, pp. 32–95.

# Index of Themes and Ideas